RACE,
LOVE,
AND
LABOR

Samuel Dorsky Museum of Art
State University of New York at New Paltz
New Paltz, New York
August 27–December 14, 2014

The Tremaine Gallery
The Hotchkiss School
Lakeville, Connecticut
February 3–March 3, 2015

University Art Museum
University at Albany
State University of New York
Albany, New York
February 2–April 2, 2016

Paul W. Zuccaire Gallery
Staller Center for the Arts
Stony Brook University
Stony Brook, New York
September 12–October 21, 2017

Published by the Samuel Dorsky Museum of Art, State University of New York at New Paltz,
on the occasion of the exhibition *Race, Love, and Labor: New Work from the Center for
Photography at Woodstock's Artist-in-Residency Program*, curated by Sarah Lewis. Original
design and printing was funded by the Howard Greenberg Endowment at The Dorsky Museum.

The Dorsky Museum's exhibitions and programs are supported by the Friends of the
Samuel Dorsky Museum of Art and the State University of New York at New Paltz.

The Center for Photography at Woodstock's Artist-in-Residency Program is supported by the
Milton & Sally Avery Arts Foundation; the National Endowment for the Arts; the New York
State Council on the Arts, a state agency; the Phillip & Edith Leonian Foundation;
The Andy Warhol Foundation for the Visual Arts; and the Thompson Family Foundation.

Designed by William van Roden
Edited by Daniel Belasco, Curator of Exhibitions and Programs,
Samuel Dorsky Museum of Art, State University of New York at New Paltz
Printed by Lightning Source
Distributed by the State University of New York Press
(www.sunypress.edu)
10 9 8 7 6 5 4 3 2

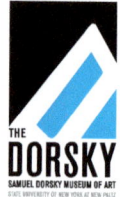 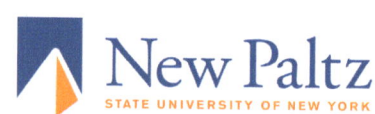 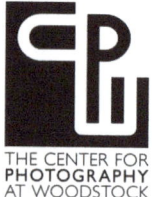

RACE, LOVE, AND LABOR

NEW WORK FROM THE CENTER FOR PHOTOGRAPHY AT WOODSTOCK'S ARTIST-IN-RESIDENCY PROGRAM

SARAH LEWIS,
EXHIBITION CURATOR

WITH CONTRIBUTIONS BY
SARA J. PASTI AND ARIEL SHANBERG

SAMUEL DORSKY MUSEUM OF ART
STATE UNIVERSITY OF
NEW YORK AT NEW PALTZ

RACE,
LOVE,
AND
LABOR

CONTENTS

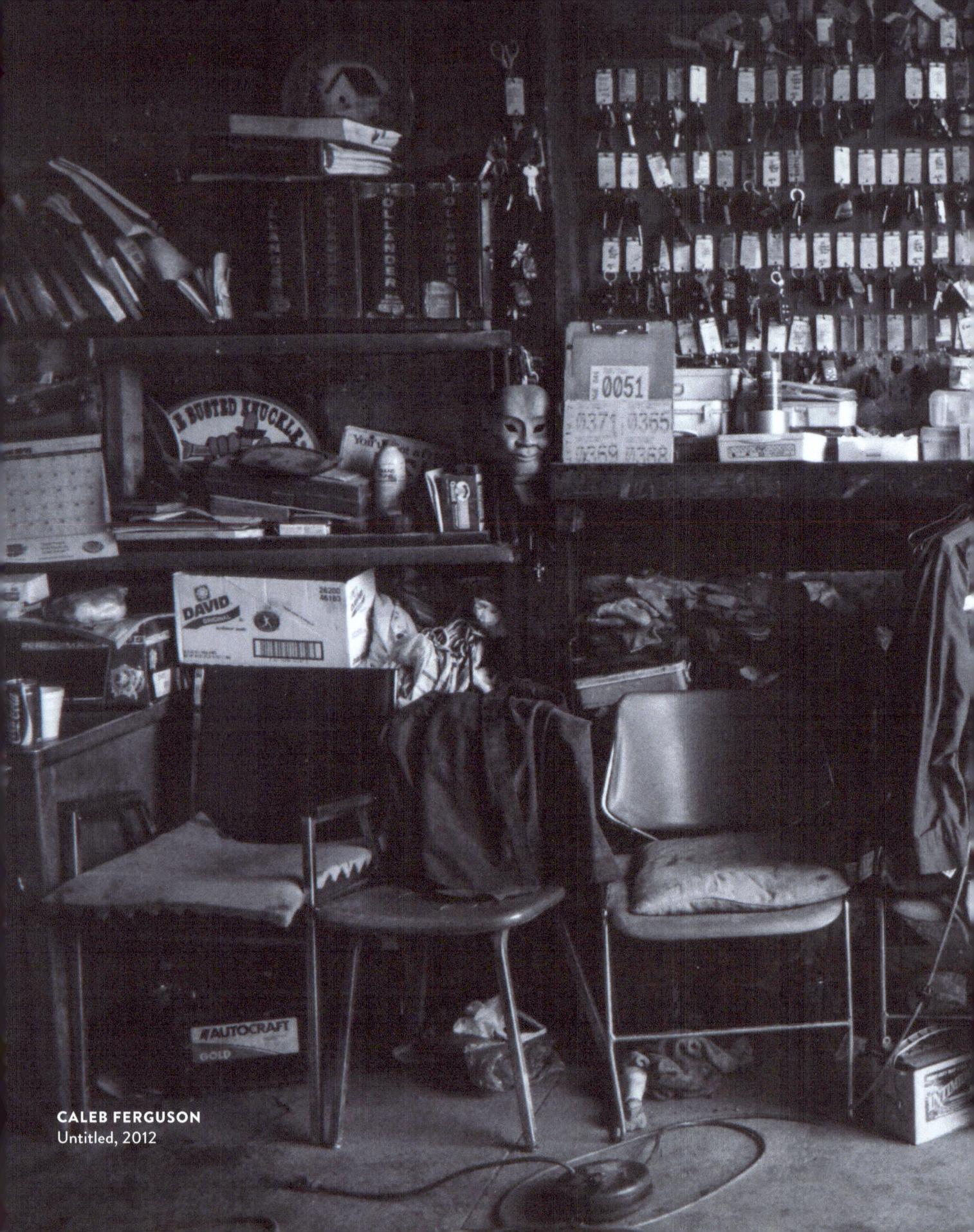

CALEB FERGUSON
Untitled, 2012

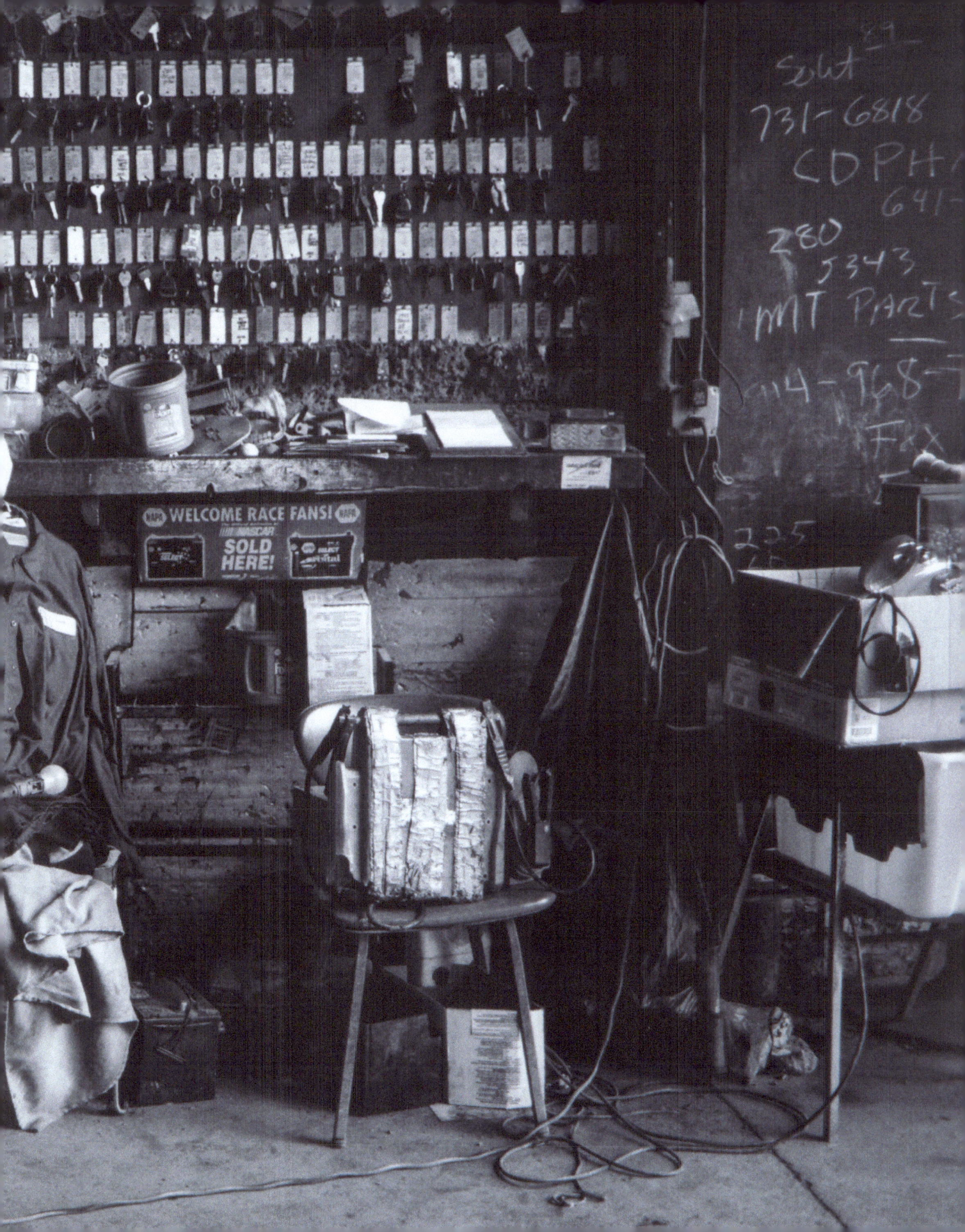

THE DORSKY AND THE CENTER FOR PHOTOGRAPHY AT WOODSTOCK:
A 20-YEAR PARTNERSHIP

SARA J. PASTI
THE NEIL C. TRAGER DIRECTOR,
SAMUEL DORSKY MUSEUM OF ART

RACE, LOVE, AND LABOR: *New Work from the Center for Photography at Woodstock's Artist-in-Residency Program* is the latest in a series of exhibitions presented by the Samuel Dorsky Museum of Art that have been drawn from the Center for Photography at Woodstock's permanent collection.

These exhibitions have their genesis in The Dorsky's longstanding relationship with CPW, which began in June 1995 when Neil C. Trager, the director of the SUNY New Paltz College Art Gallery, invited Colleen Kenyon, the director of the Center for Photography at Woodstock, to place CPW's permanent collection on long-term loan to the College Art Gallery. As a result of that invitation, CPW delivered 895 photographs to the SUNY New Paltz campus, launching a relationship that has been going strong for twenty years.

The partnership achieves several goals, primary among them the safekeeping of CPW's excellent collection of photographs. In addition, the loan expands public access to the photographs and allows them to be catalogued, studied, and exhibited on an ongoing basis. Since their transfer to SUNY New Paltz, the photographs have been widely used by SUNY New Paltz photography and art history professors to show examples of modern photographic processes. The collection has also been studied by photography classes from New Paltz High School, Highland High School, and the Newburgh Free Academy.

Numerous exhibitions at SUNY New Paltz have featured photographs from CPW's collection. Since 2001, The Dorsky Museum exhibitions have been: *Engaging Pictures: Aesthetic Choices from the Center for Photography at Woodstock* (2001); *Center for Photography at Woodstock: 25 Years of Imaging* (2002); *Interpreting Utopia* (2007); *All Hot and Bothered: Photographs from the Center for Photography at Woodstock* (2008); *Thoughts of Home: Photographs from the Center for Photography at Woodstock Permanent Collection* (2011); and *Linking Collections, Building Connections: Works from the Hudson Valley Visual Art Consortium Collections* (2011).

Though the photography collections owned by CPW and The Dorsky have been stored side-by-side for many years, they have developed independently. The Dorsky now has a very strong collection of 19th and early and mid 20th century photographs while CPW's collection is largely contemporary, featuring work by artists from the latter part of the 20th and the early 21st centuries. Viewed together, the two collections provide audiences on campus and beyond with a strong overview of the history of photography.

The current exhibition and its catalogue celebrate both the 20-year relationship between SUNY New Paltz and the Center for Photography at Woodstock and the 15th anniversary of CPW's Artist-in-Residency Program, described later in the catalogue by Ariel Shanberg,

CPW's executive director. Participants in the WOODSTOCK A-I-R donate one or more prints to CPW's permanent collection, forming a unique body of work that captures the shifting currents of contemporary photographic practices.

For their help with this project, I wish to thank the SUNY New Paltz Foundation; the State University of New York at New Paltz; the staff and Friends of The Dorsky Museum—in particular, Daniel Belasco, curator of exhibitions and programs, Wayne Lempka, collections manager, Janis Benincasa, programs manager, Jessica Longobardo, graduate assistant, Amy Pickering, visitor services coordinator, and Bob Wagner, preparator; and the staff and board of the Center for Photography at Woodstock—in particular, executive director Ariel Shanberg and collections intern Jonas Caulfield. William van Roden designed this impressive catalogue. I also wish to thank Howard Greenberg, the founder of the Center for Photography at Woodstock and a generous donor of photographs to both the CPW and The Dorsky. Without Howard, none of this would have been possible. Finally, special thanks go to Sarah Lewis, the exhibition's curator, for her excellent work in organizing this presentation which sheds light on the outstanding photographs, video, and artist books produced through CPW's Artist-in-Residency Program.

We look forward to presenting many more exhibitions of work from the Center for Photography at Woodstock in the years ahead and to continuing and expanding our long-standing collaboration.

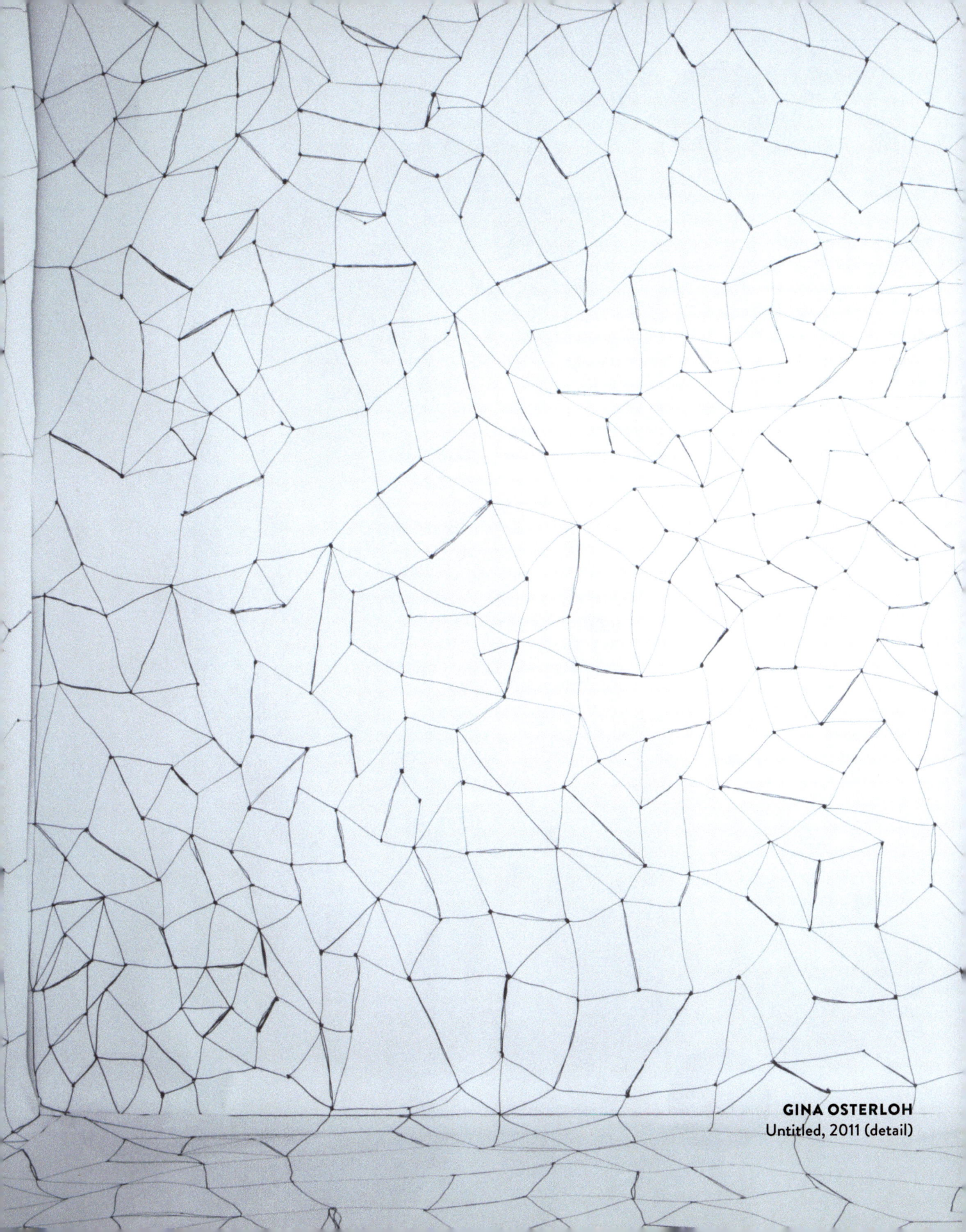

GINA OSTERLOH
Untitled, 2011 (detail)

THE WORK OF MAKING ART

ARIEL SHANBERG
EXECUTIVE DIRECTOR,
THE CENTER FOR PHOTOGRAPHY AT WOODSTOCK

WHAT TAKES PLACE DURING an artist workspace residency is sacred. Defined by the philosophy of unhindered creativity and singular focus, such a period of time is rare and precious. As the 21st century beckons us to keep pace with the multitasking abilities of the devices that propel our daily lives, the stillness found within the guarded time provided by an artist residency is a priceless gift.

Art making is intrinsically tied to Woodstock's identity. As the "Colony of the Arts," the town of Woodstock has a long tradition of inspiring, nurturing, and supporting artists and their creative practices. The Center for Photography at Woodstock (CPW) is part of a vibrant legacy, which includes the Byrdcliffe Art Colony (where CPW's residents lived from 1999–2009), the Maverick Colony, the Woodstock Artists Association and Museum, and the Woodstock School of Art. Since CPW was founded in 1977, it has committed to providing an artistic home for photographers in the region and beyond.

With the creation in 1999 of WOODSTOCK A-I-R, an artist workspace residency program for artists of color working in the photographic arts, the original vision of CPW as an artistic home was most fully articulated. The program's particular mission—to support artists of color—was forged with the goal to level the playing field and broaden the ranks of those who partake in the artist residency tradition. WOODSTOCK A-I-R ensures that our region, which has inspired artists for over a century, will be accessible to all. The diversity CPW's artists-in-residence bring to this region and their participation in its legacy deeply enriches the region and ensures its continuity.

CPW's artists-in-residence are encouraged to break new ground and deepen their commitment to their creative practices, with the support of a dedicated staff—all artists themselves. For many of its participants, WOODSTOCK A-I-R has marked their first workspace residency experience—a time in which they are solely recognized as an artist and given the time, space, and means to be one, 24/7. The lasting value of a residency should not be measured solely by the production of new art works, but by the cumulative growth that results and is articulated through an expansion of creative vision. Achieving that involves taking risks, exploring uncharted territories, and asking questions, not necessarily seeking answers. The works of art that ultimately emerge from the experience, whether created on-site or years later, reflect the tremendous impact of a successful artist workspace residency.

Many of the activities surrounding an artist workspace residency are unseen by the public. To form a public record of WOODSTOCK A-I-R, CPW has collected works made by its artists. The over 1,800 works in the collection—which also includes works by artists who have exhibited at CPW, led workshops, been published in CPW's journal, *Photography Quarterly*, or received the annual Photographers' Fellowship Fund, as well as prints donated by generous patrons—offer keen insight into nearly four decades of artists working in photography at the onset of their professional careers. It is a history within the history of photography. Often CPW is one of the first public collections to acquire work by these artists. In collecting, we are creating a record of their activities as well as elevating their visibility, connecting them with new audiences in the present and years to come.

The ongoing 20-year partnership with the Samuel Dorsky Museum of Art at SUNY New Paltz allows that exposure to happen in ways simply not possible for a small independent organization. We are indebted to the vision held by The Dorsky's founding director Neil C. Trager and CPW's former director Colleen Kenyon as well as the deep ongoing commitment of The Dorsky director Sara Pasti, collections manager Wayne Lempka, curator of exhibitions Daniel Belasco, and the rest of the museum's staff. The foresight for starting the collection came from CPW's founder, Howard Greenberg. No expression of gratitude could fully measure his impact.

I would like to take this opportunity to acknowledge and thank the many CPW staff members who have helped make each residency a defining experience over the years: Colleen Kenyon and Kitty McCullough whose vision for the program and 1998 NEA grant application kick-started the program; Rachel Cohen, Judi Esmond, Megan Flaherty, Liz Glynn, Mark Harley, Akemi Hiatt, Rose Jerome, Kathleen Kenyon, Larry Lewis, Phil Mansfield, Kate Menconeri, Lindsay Stern, and Liz Unterman; and countless interns whose contributions to our A-I-Rs have left an indelible mark.

CPW's participation in the New York State Artist Workspace Consortium from 2004–2009, led by Elizabeth Merena and Kerry McCarthy, was a transformative experience, which has deepened this organization's commitment to supporting artists indelibly.

WOODSTOCK A-I-R has been fortunate to have the steadfast support of a number of funders over the years including the New York State Council on the Arts, the National Endowment for the Arts, the Andy Warhol Foundation for the Visual Arts, the André & Elisabeth Kertész Foundation, the Milton & Sally Avery Arts Foundation, the Phillip and Edith Leonian Foundation, and the Wade A. Thompson Foundation, as well as from CPW's Board of Directors.

And finally my thanks to Sarah Lewis for generously bringing her exceptional talents to this collaboration and curating this exhibition. A collection's true value is appraised only when it is seen anew—when those who cull through and interpret its holdings bring to light new meaning and importance within the present day. The dialogue Sarah brings forth in *Race, Love, and Labor* does that and more.

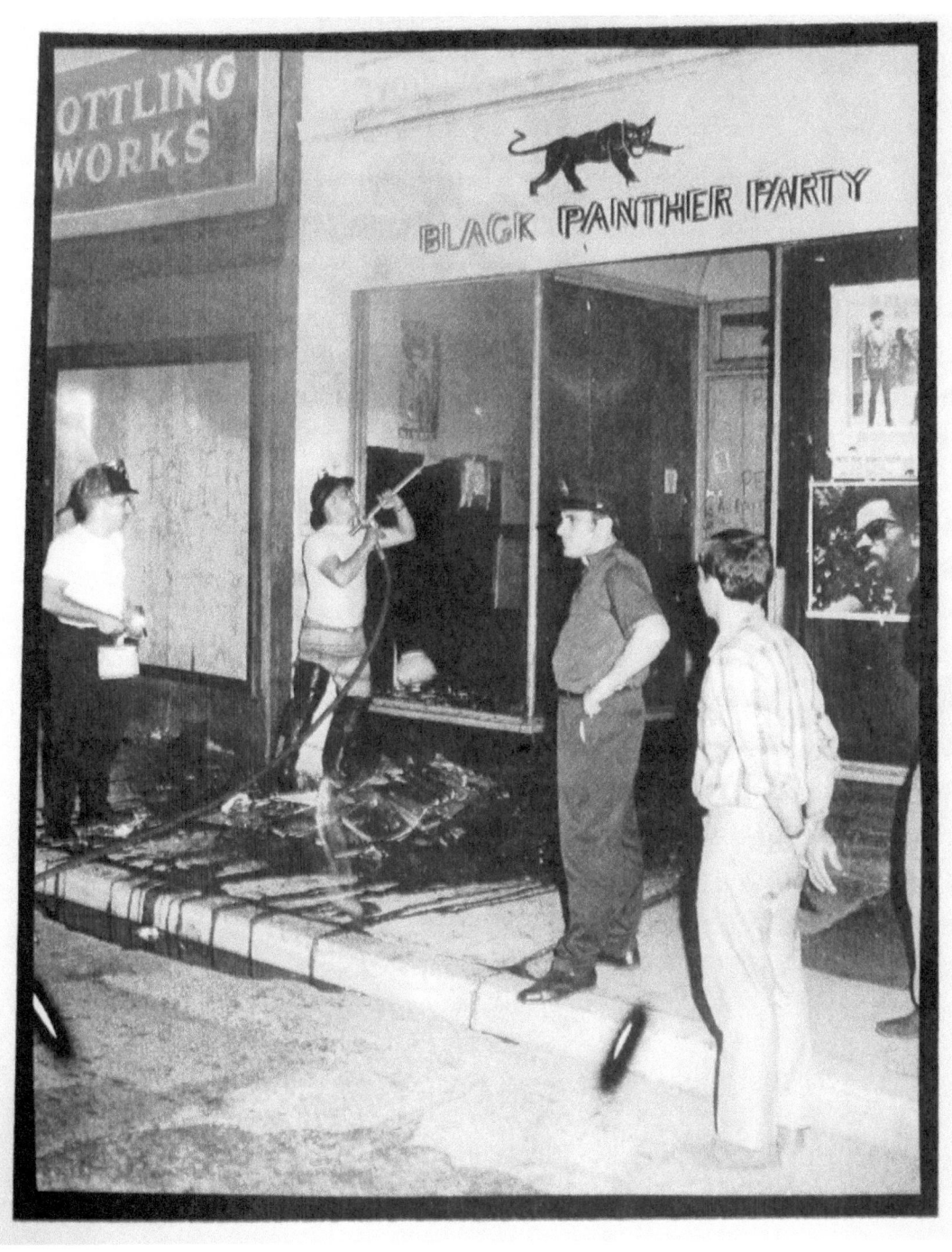

WILLIAM CORDOVA
Albany/Peekskill (detail), 2007

RACE, LOVE, AND LABOR:
NEW WORK FROM THE CENTER FOR PHOTOGRAPHY AT WOODSTOCK

SARAH LEWIS
EXHIBITION CURATOR

IF I COULD DO IT, I'D DO NO WRITING AT ALL HERE. IT WOULD BE PHOTOGRAPHS; THE REST WOULD BE FRAGMENTS OF CLOTH, BITS OF COTTON, LUMPS OF EARTH, RECORDS OF SPEECH, PIECES OF WOOD AND IRON . . . —JAMES AGEE

IT IS IMPOSSIBLE TO SEPARATE the history of photography from the history of labor, love, and race in America. At the advent of photography, a deal was struck: the medium would document both the intimacies we cherish and their cost in human toil. It is a paradox that Frederick Douglass would remind us of during the Civil War: photographs were instruments used to erase part of the human family and it would take images of human dignity and determination to rectify it. The labor of photography is to wrestle with this legacy. It is not work but labor: a means through which we birth ourselves anew.

This exhibition, culled from the collection of the Center for Photography at Woodstock's Artist-in-Residency program, displays images by artists who understand the needs of labor in the fullest sense of the word. They are part of a 15-year-old tradition at the Center for Photography at Woodstock, which offers artists of color one of the requirements for a sterling creative practice—embryonic time to probe deeply, unfettered by distractions. At the 20th anniversary of the Center for Photography's partnership with the Samuel Dorsky Museum of Art at SUNY New Paltz, it is a moment to not only honor this residency, but to examine the themes that have emerged from the resulting, irreplaceable pictures.

A reflective look at the CPW collection shows how photographers, working with a vast range of aesthetics, play a critical role in the labor of becoming and the work it entails—on the land and within our inner worlds. This exhibition includes a range of such photographs, from pictures by LaToya Ruby Frazier, whose fierce portrayals of the consequences of work on wellbeing and human dignity sears the soul with a light that Walker Evans could have never anticipated, to images by Deana Lawson who expertly shows a hard won self-possession through her pioneering portrayal of nude forms. Here too are images of the full landscape of self-determination movements. In William Cordova's photographs of archival materials, it is as if an archeologist has found the Black Panthers and Young Lords in both sites and hidden sights in Peekskill and Albany, NY. Gina Osterloh's pen-and-ink fabricated triptych shows us what comes of will and determination of another kind—the will required to create an inner landscape of ambitions.

What unites these images is an animating sense of what it means to live in this lineage of photography's paradox—to reduce and to exult. These photographs, the gift of a moment in time through a unique residency, show us where a future path may lead. My gratitude goes to my three colleagues—Dorsky director Sara Pasti, Dorsky curator of exhibitions Daniel Belasco, and the executive director of the Center for Photography at Woodstock, Ariel Shanberg—for the honor of organizing this show, and to the artists for entrusting me to present their images as a new constellation.

PLATES

ENDIA BEAL
(b. United States, 1985)
9 to 5 (still), 2014
HD video, sound
3 min.
The Center for Photography at Woodstock
Permanent Print Collection 2014.013

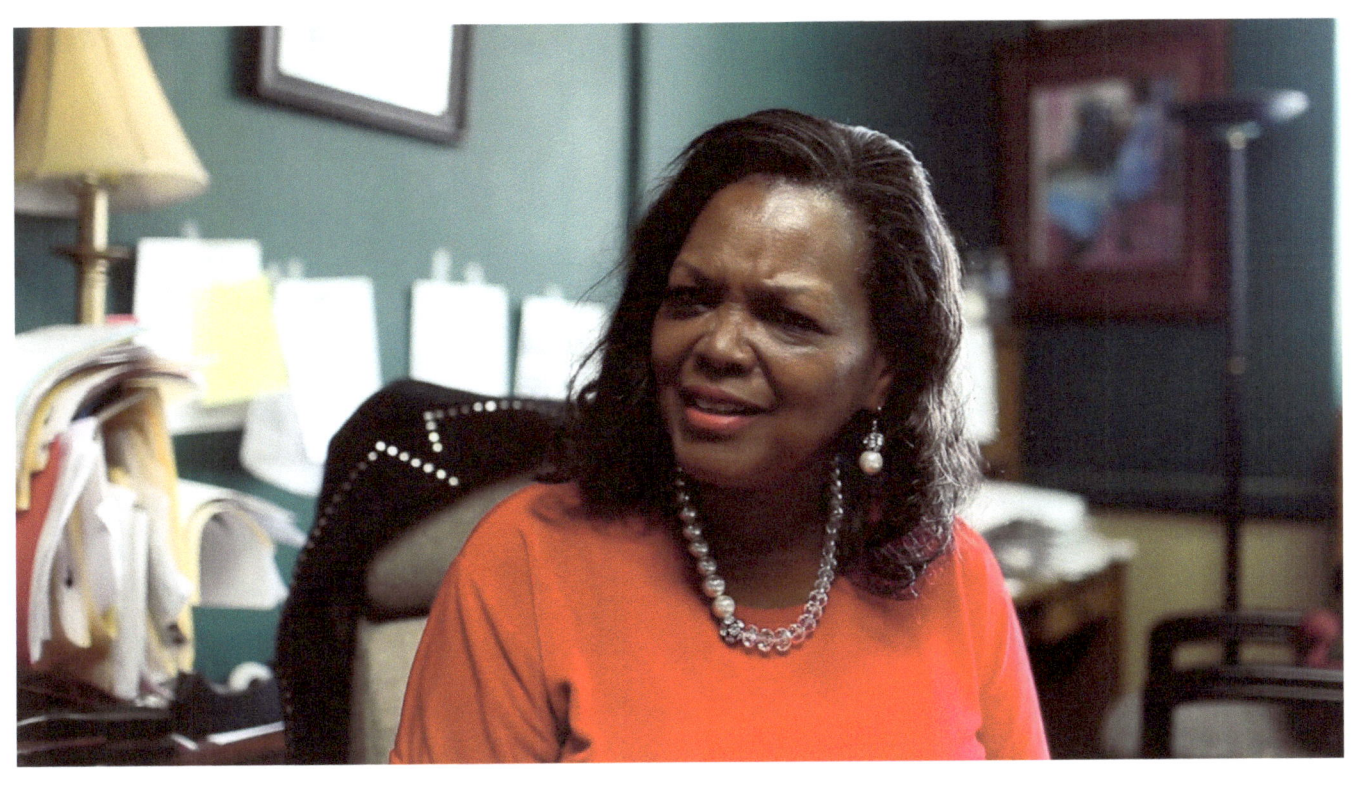

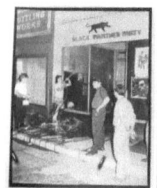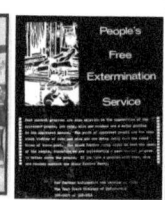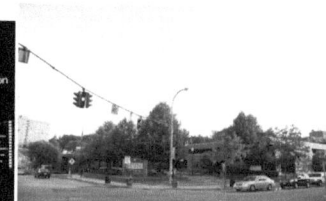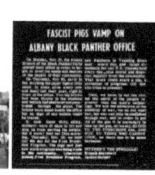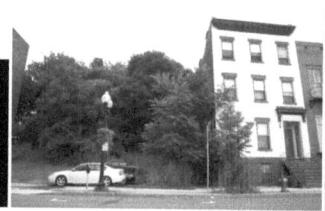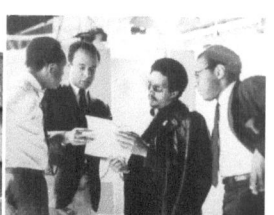

WILLIAM CORDOVA
(b. Peru, 1971)
Albany/Peekskill (from the series "chapters:
making the invisible visible"), 2007
Archival pigment prints
14 parts, 14 ¼ in. x 13 ft. 5 in. overall
The Center for Photography at Woodstock
Permanent Print Collection 2014.012

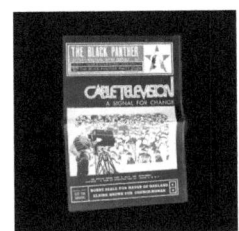 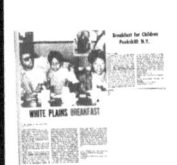 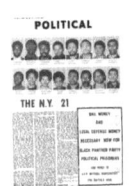 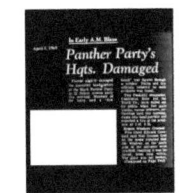 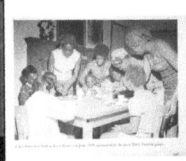 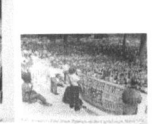 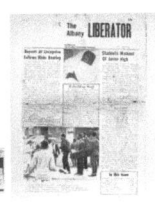

ISAAC DIGGS
(b. United States, 1972)
Untitled (Couple at Table), 2011
Archival pigment print
13 x 19 ¼ in.
The Center for Photography at Woodstock
Permanent Print Collection 2011.004

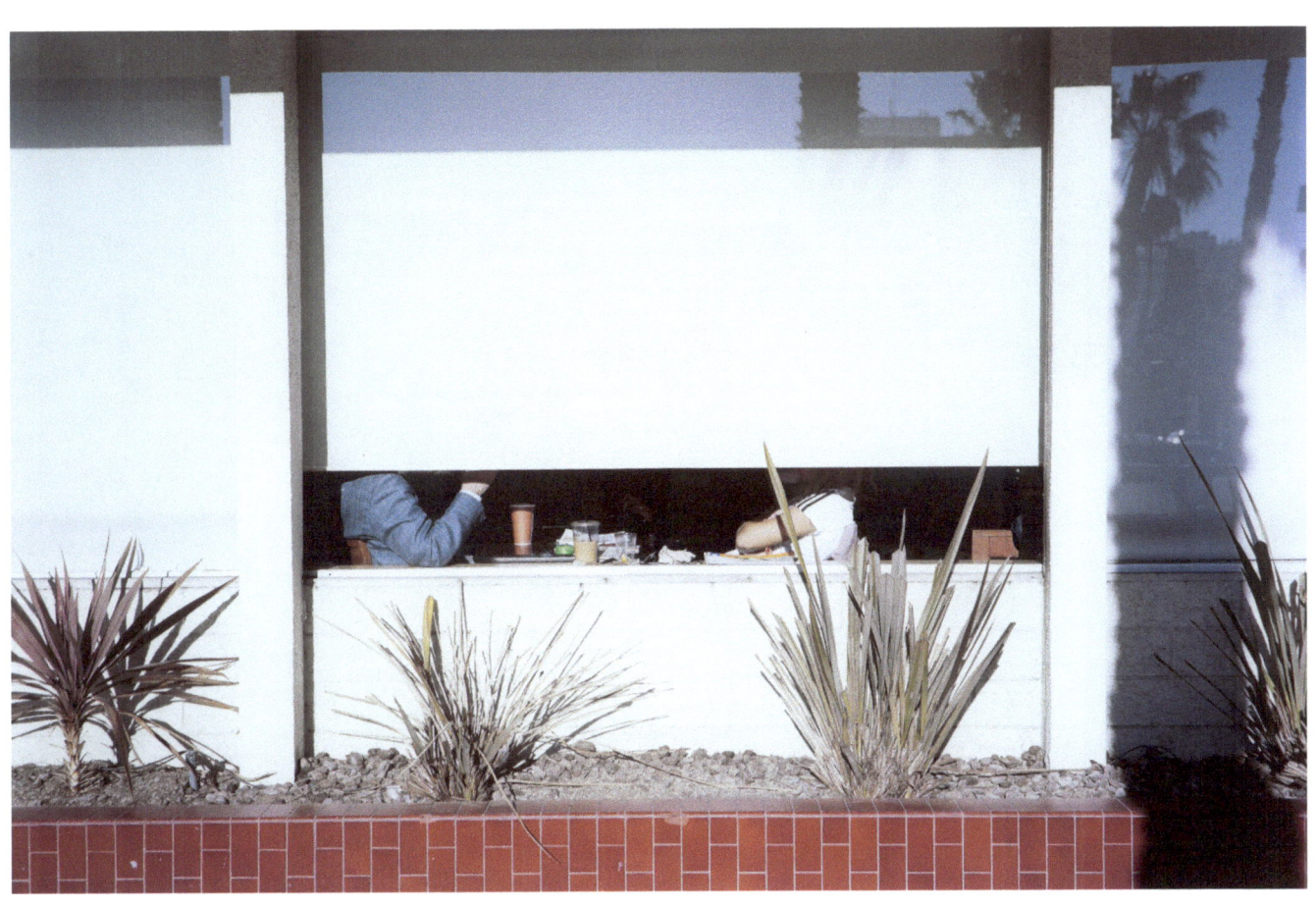

CALEB FERGUSON
(b. United States, 1986)
Untitled, 2012
Archival pigment print
8 x 12 in.
The Center for Photography at Woodstock
Permanent Print Collection 2014.006

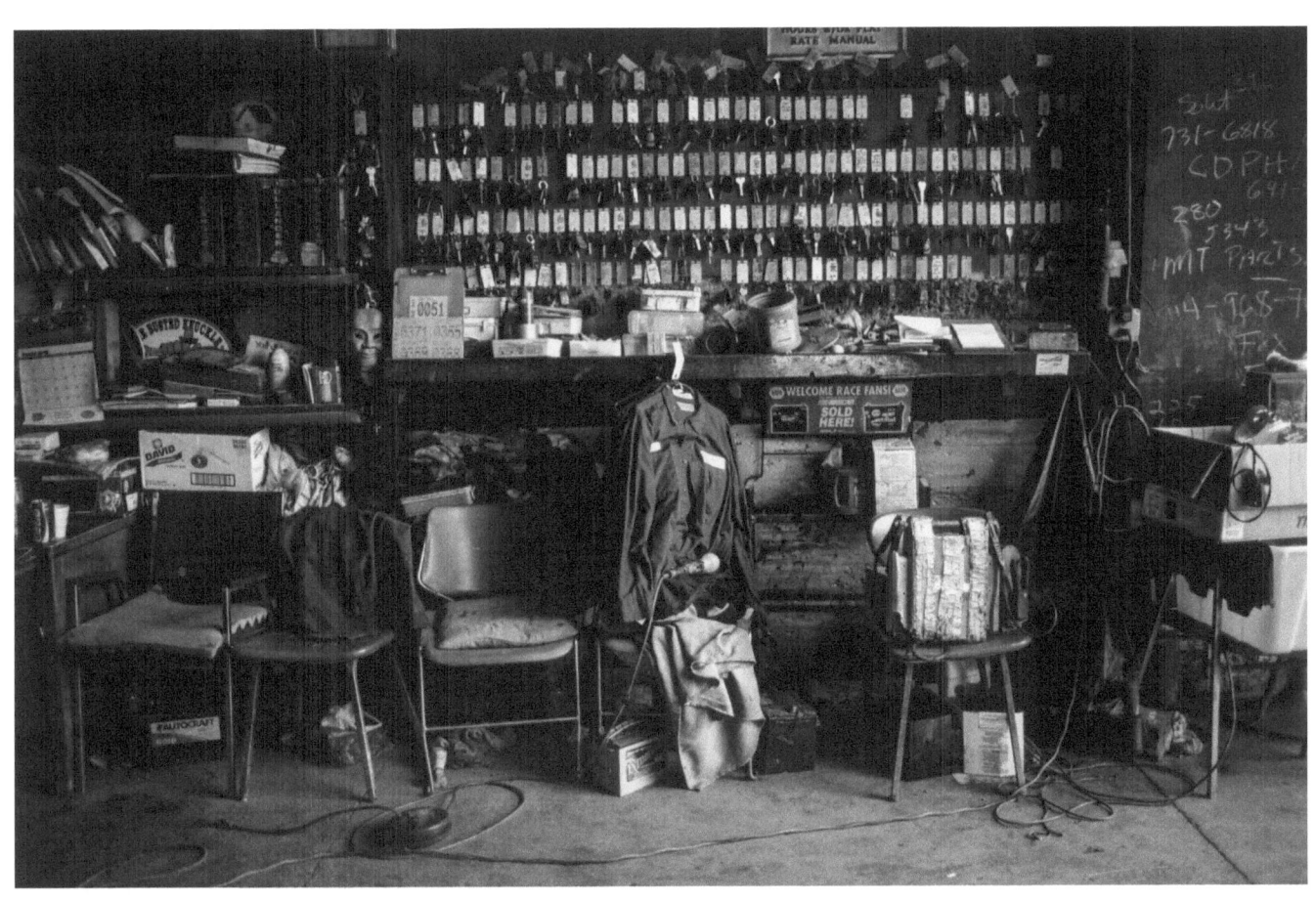

CALEB FERGUSON
(b. United States, 1986)
Untitled, 2012
Archival pigment print
8 x 12 in.
The Center for Photography at Woodstock
Permanent Print Collection 2014.003

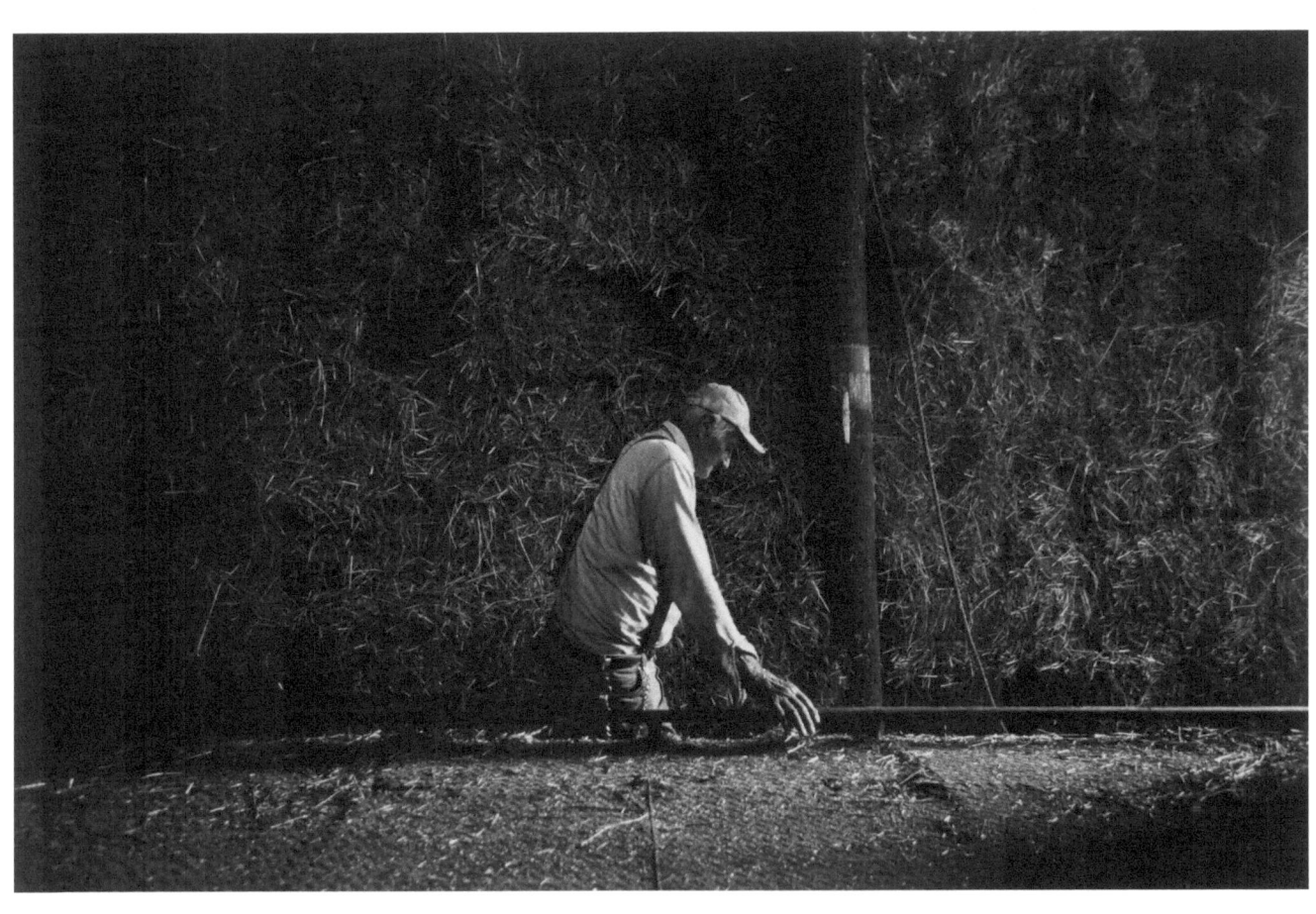

LATOYA RUBY FRAZIER
(b. United States, 1982)
Momme (from the series "The Notion of Family:
Family Work 2002–2008"), 2008
Gelatin silver print
14 ⅝ x 18 ¼ in.
The Center for Photography at Woodstock
Permanent Print Collection 2010.096

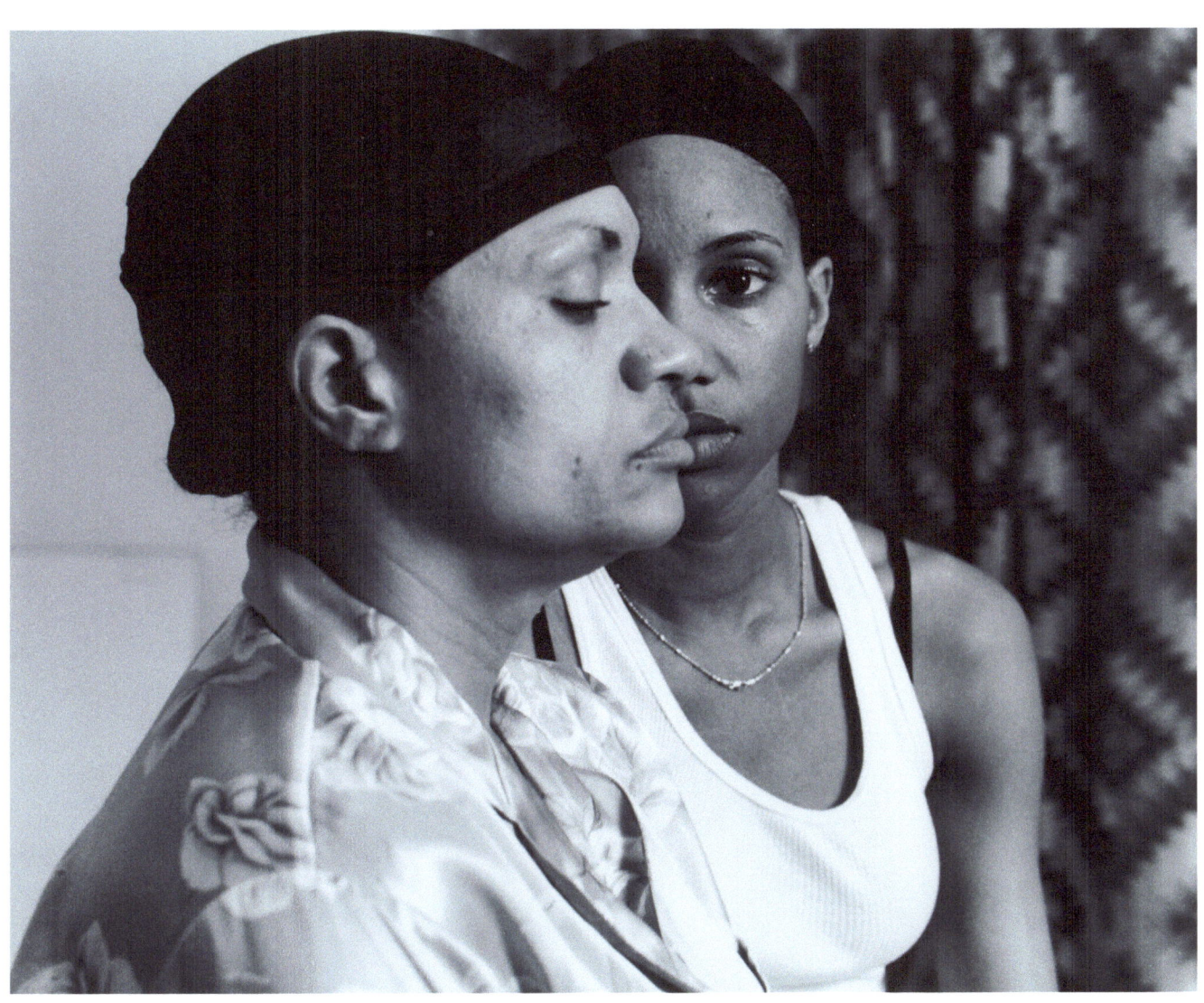

LATOYA RUBY FRAZIER
(b. United States, 1982)
Untitled (from the series "The Notion of Family:
Family Work 2002–2008"), 2008
Gelatin silver print
14 ⅜ x 19 in.
The Center for Photography at Woodstock
Permanent Print Collection 2010.097

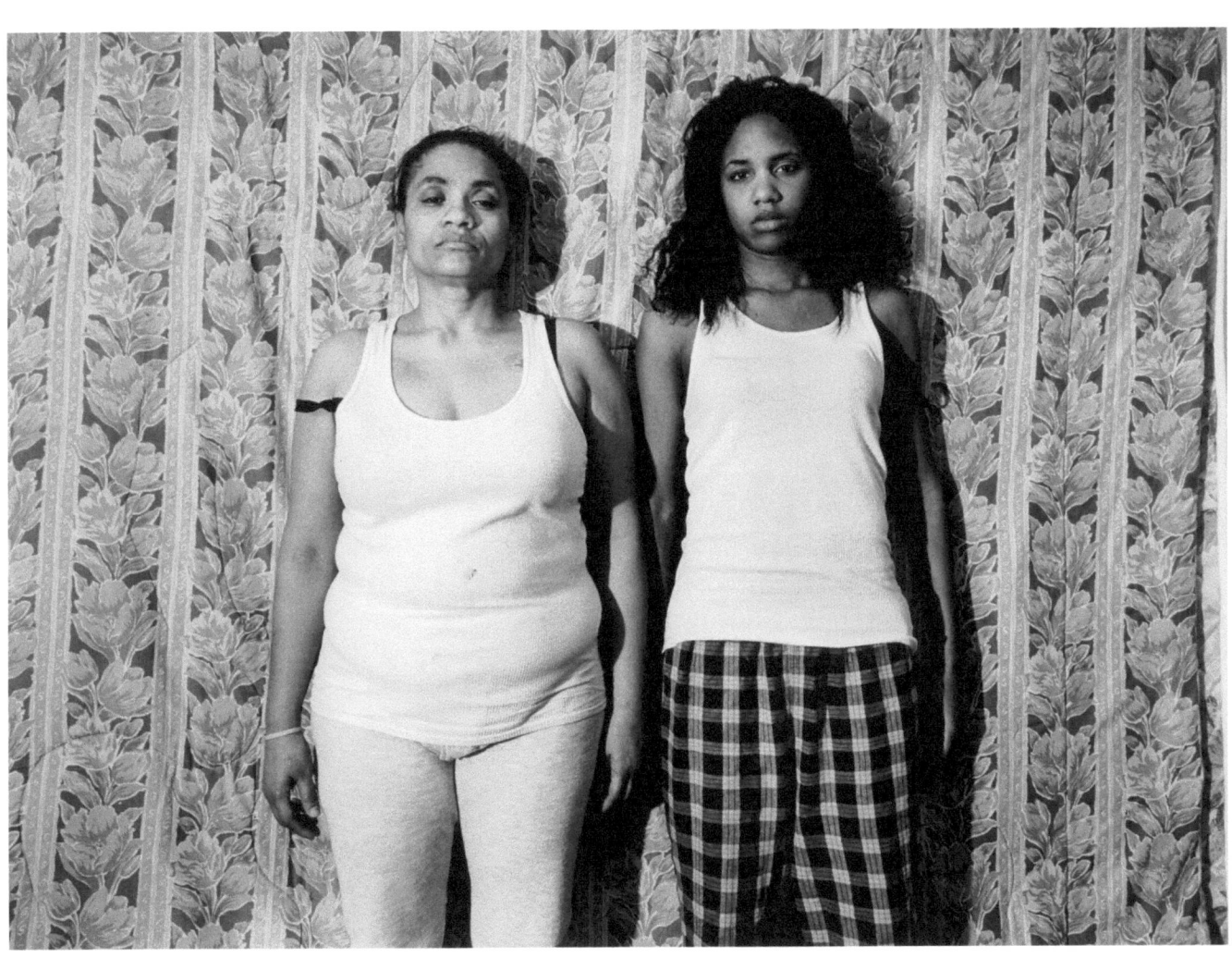

NIKITA GALE
(b. United States, 1983)
1961, 2012
Artist book
9 x 6½ x 1⅜ in. (closed)
The Center for Photography at Woodstock
Permanent Print Collection 2012.016

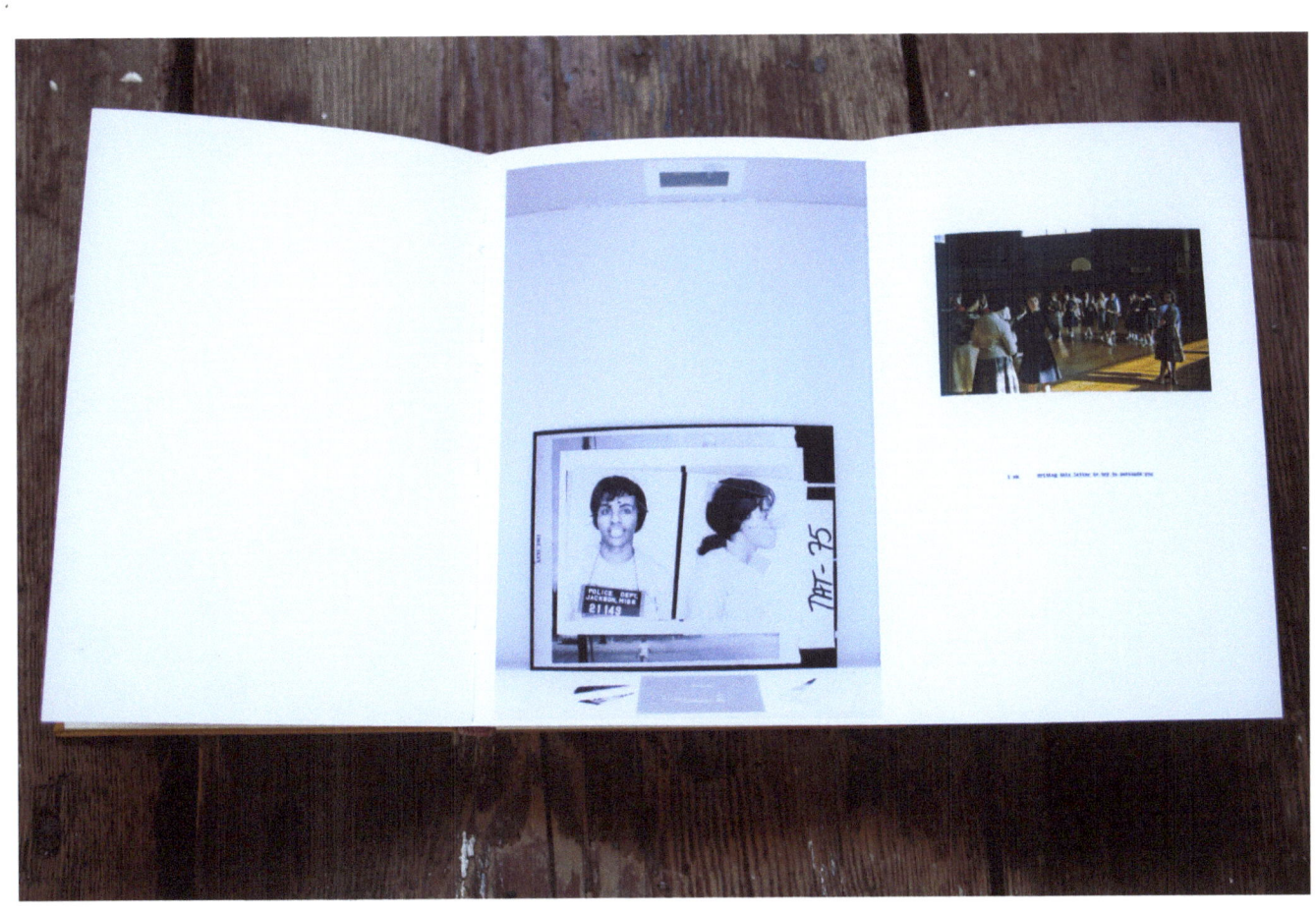

GERARD H. GASKIN
(b. Trinidad and Tobago, 1969)
Latex Ball, Manhattan, NY, 2007
(from the series "Legendary"), 2011
Archival pigment print
14 x 21 in.
The Center for Photography at Woodstock
Permanent Print Collection 2011.009

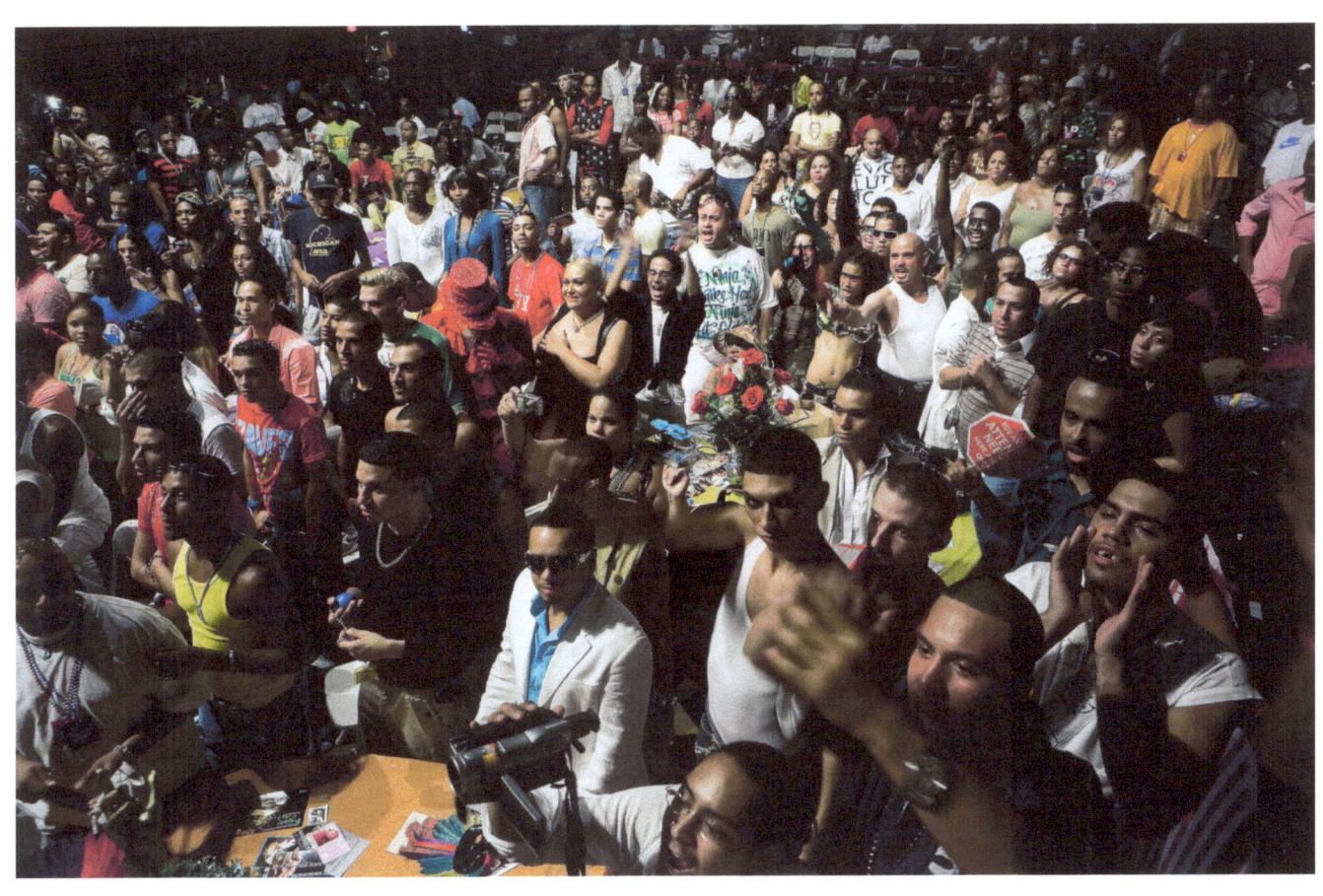

EYAKEM GULILAT
(b. Ethiopia, 1976)
Memories of My Father
(from the series "Memories"), 2010
Archival pigment print
16 x 20 in.
The Center for Photography at Woodstock
Permanent Print Collection 2011.011

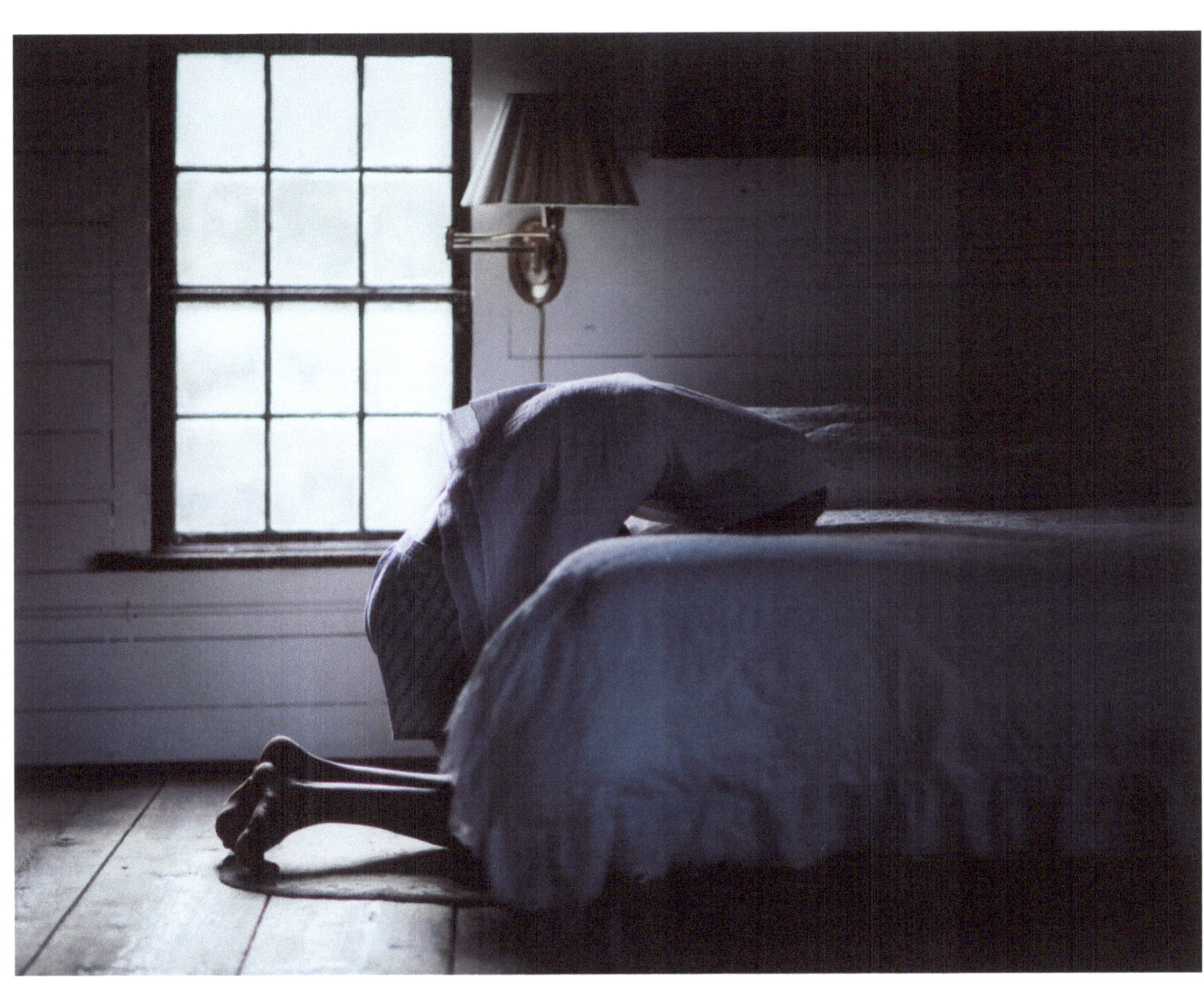

TOMMY KHA
(b. United States, 1988)
Little Polite (A Role Study), 2011
Chromogenic color print
21 ⅛ x 28 ¾ in.
The Center for Photography at Woodstock
Permanent Print Collection 2012.007

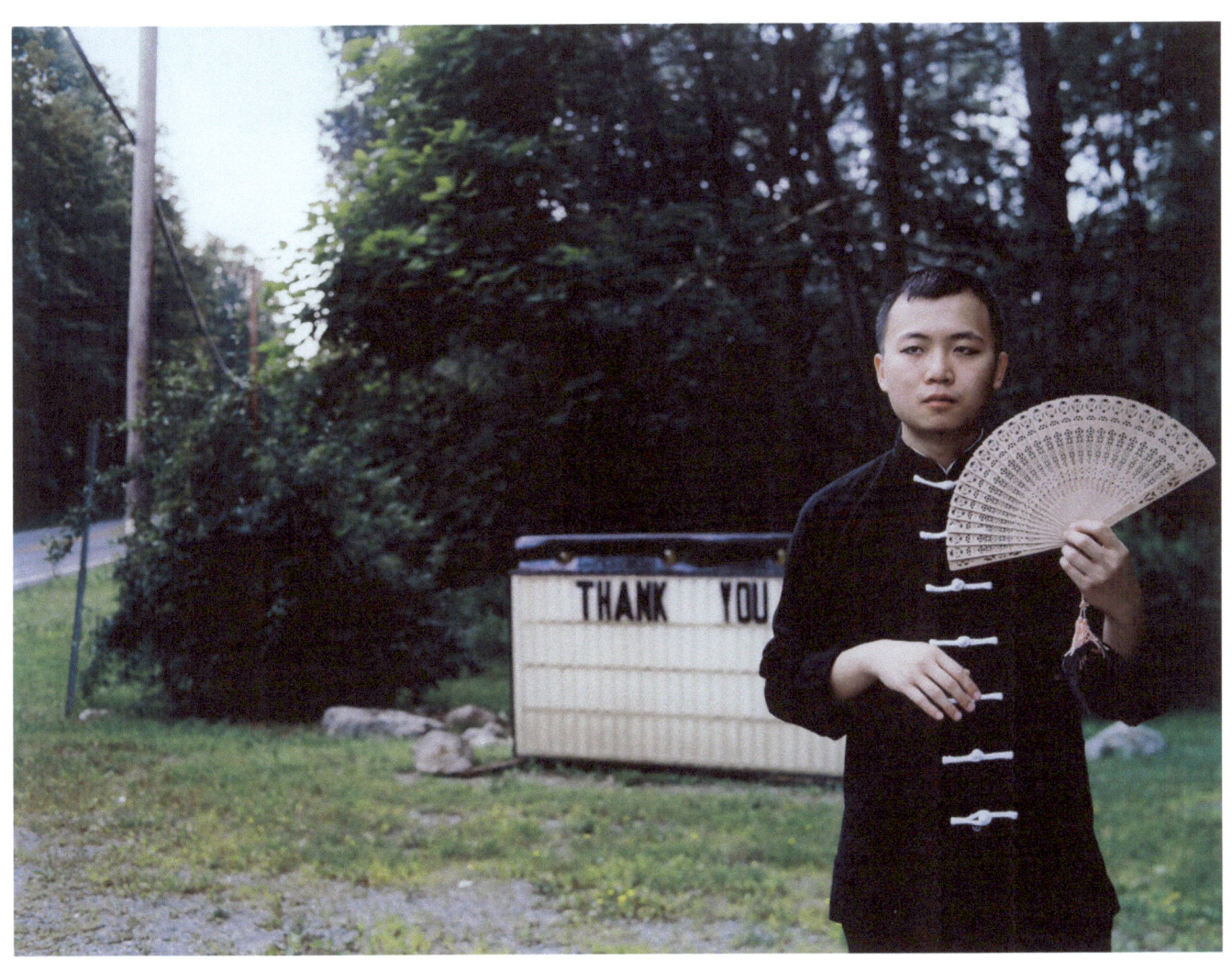

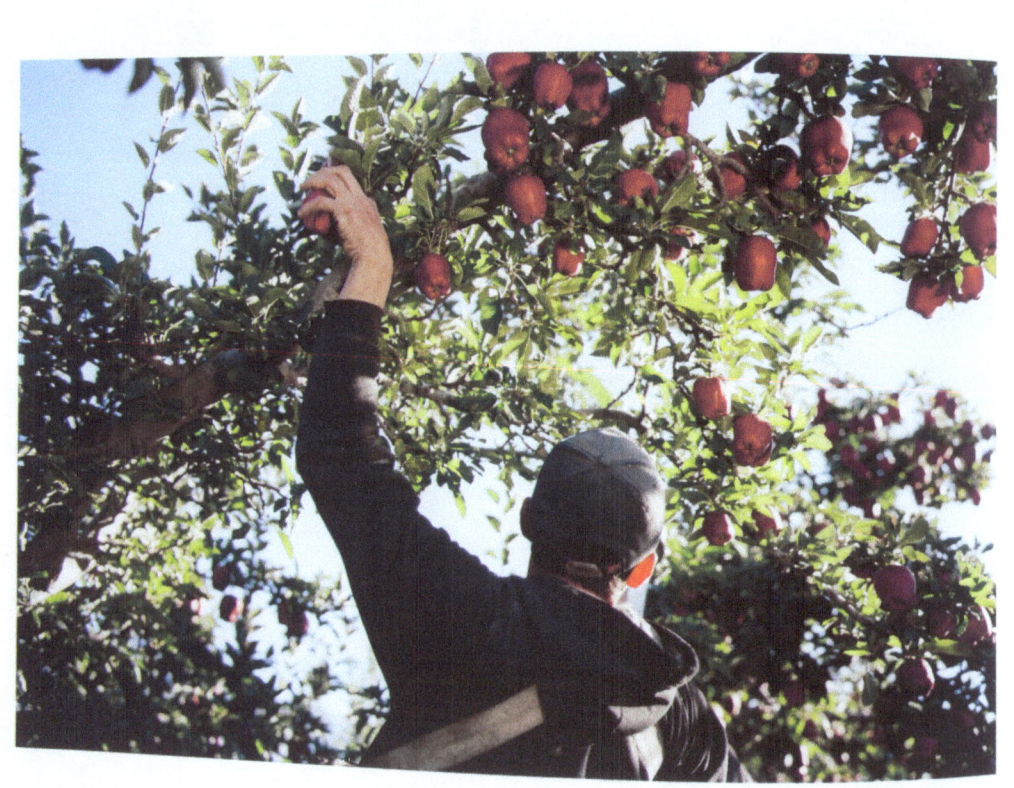

KATHYA MARIA LANDEROS
(b. United States, 1977)
Verdant Land, 2013
Artist book
13 ⅜ x 16 x ⅝ in. (closed)
The Center for Photography at Woodstock
Permanent Print Collection 2013.007

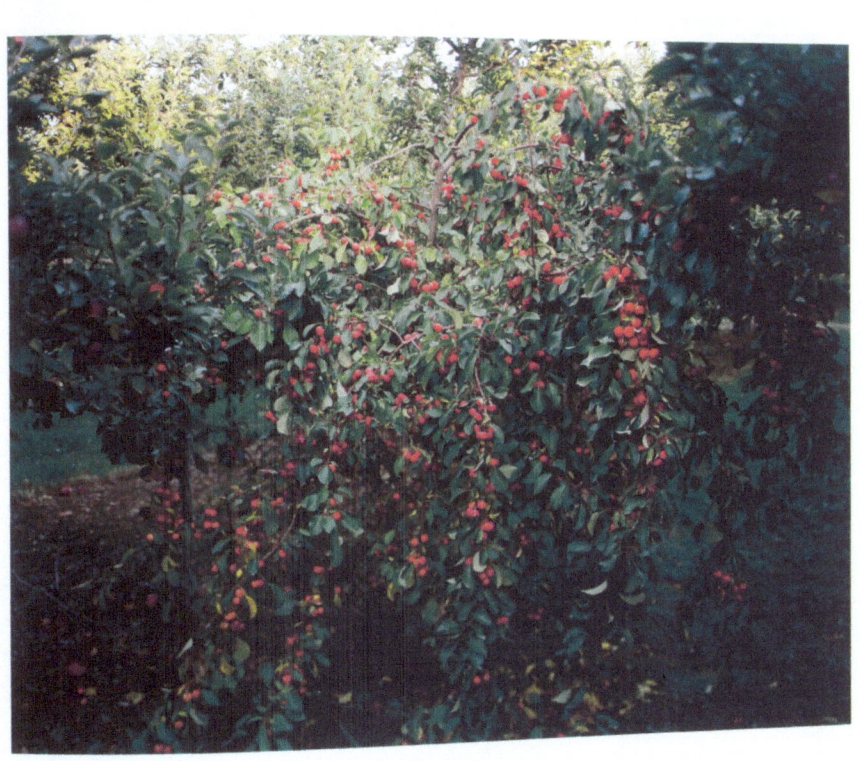

DEANA LAWSON
(b. United States, 1979)
Daonne, 2012
Archival pigment print
31 x 40 in.
The Center for Photography at Woodstock
Permanent Print Collection 2012.017

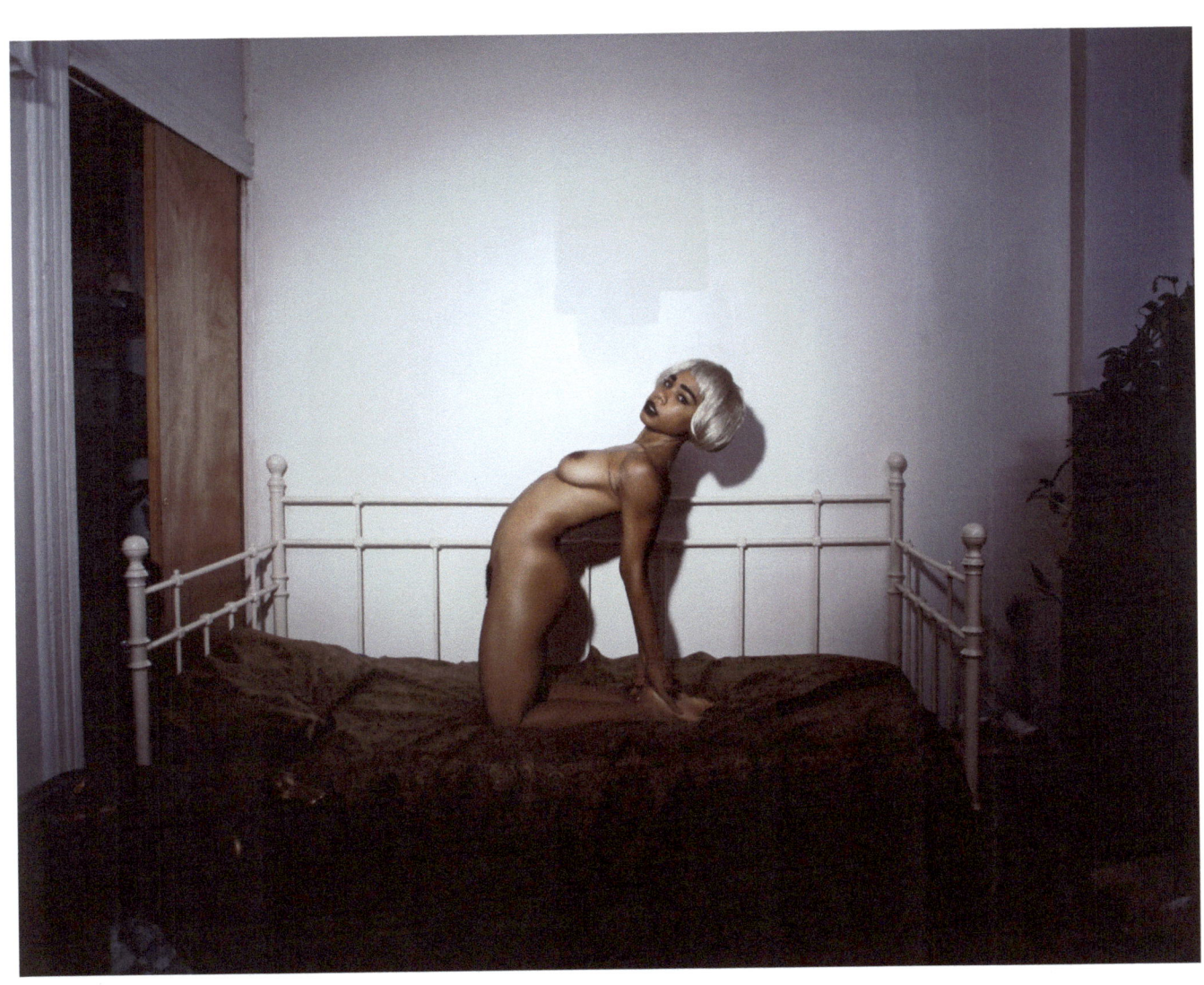

ALMA LEIVA
(b. Honduras, 1975)
Celdas #12 (from the series "Celdas (Prison Cells)"), 2012
Chromogenic color print
23 ¼ x 23 ¼ in.
The Center for Photography at Woodstock
Permanent Print Collection 2014.011

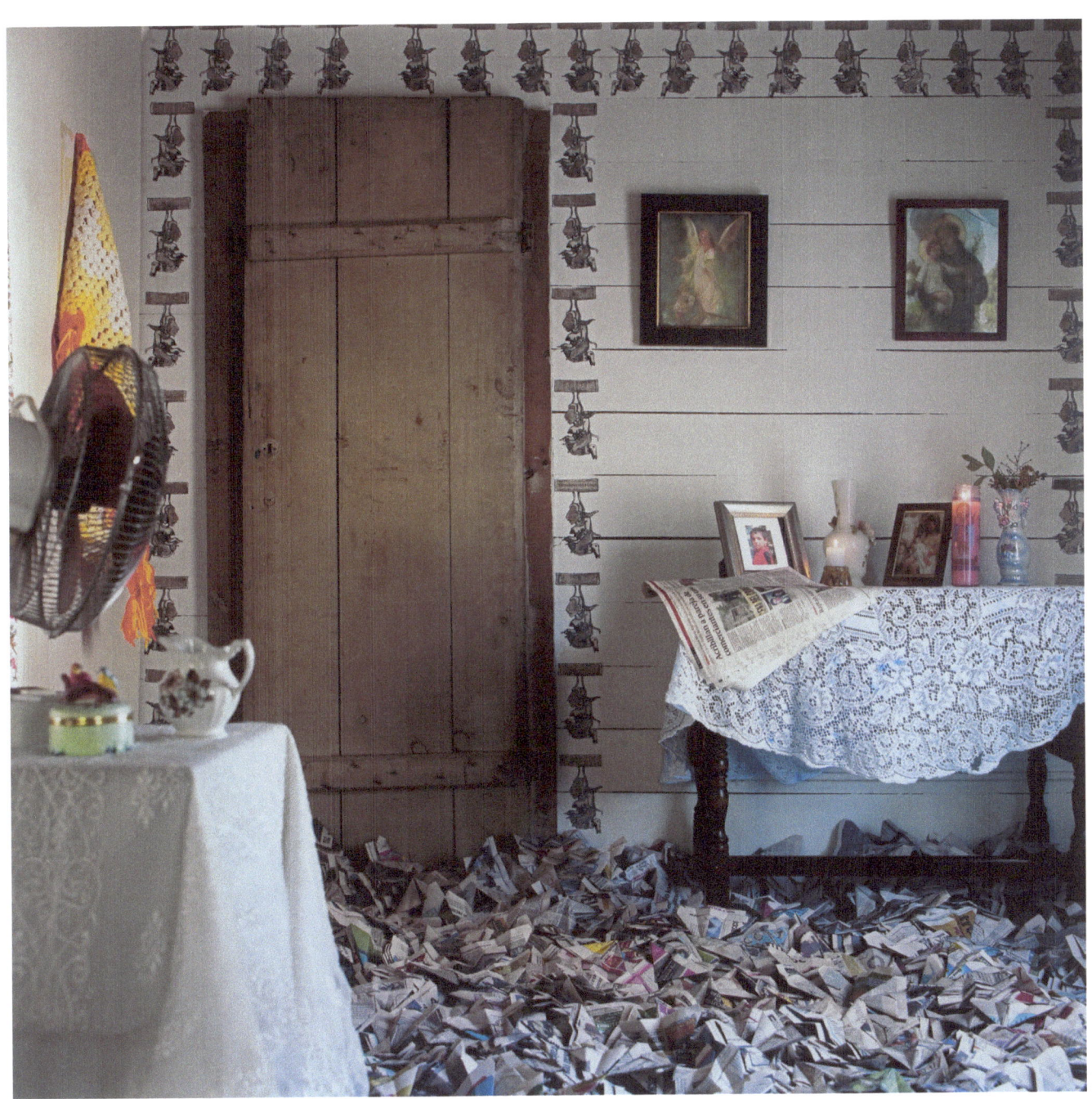

YIJUN PIXY LIAO
(b. China, 1979)
Pimo Dictionary, 2010
Artist book
6 ⅜ x 4 ¾ x ⅞ in. (closed)
The Center for Photography at Woodstock
Permanent Print Collection 2010.113

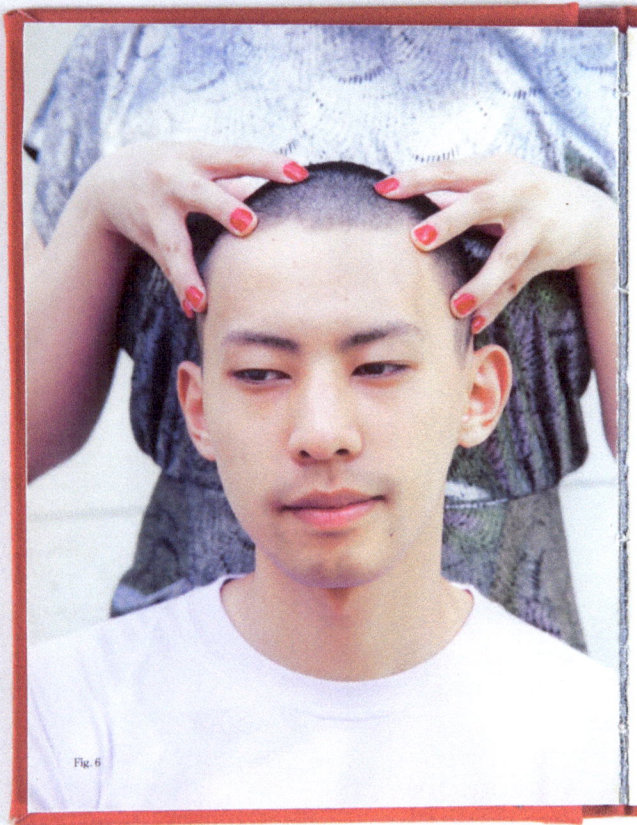

Fig. 6

H.

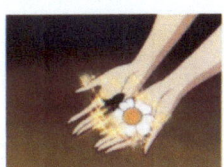

Fig. 7

Hana no Ko Lunlun
Cartoon that most influenced Pixy about a flower girl, a speaking cat and a speaking dog. (Fig. 7)

Happy Fat
Moro calls Pixy's fat "happy fat". He thinks Pixy gets fat because he is being too nice to her.

Head Orgasm
The orgasm one can get during a head message. See **Full Massage. (**Fig. 6)

Hola Hola Hola
Moro's signature line to make Pixy flush.

GINA OSTERLOH
(b. United States, 1973)
Untitled, 2011
Archival pigment prints
3 parts, 19 ¼ x 23 ¾ in. each
The Center for Photography at Woodstock
Permanent Print Collection 2012.010–012

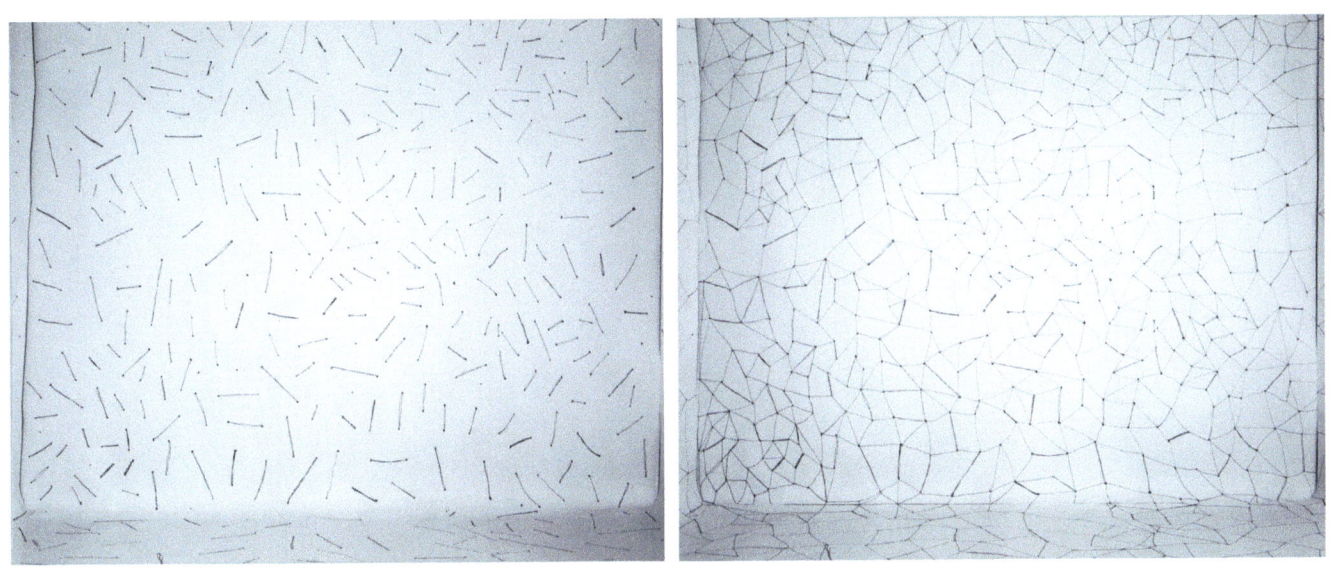

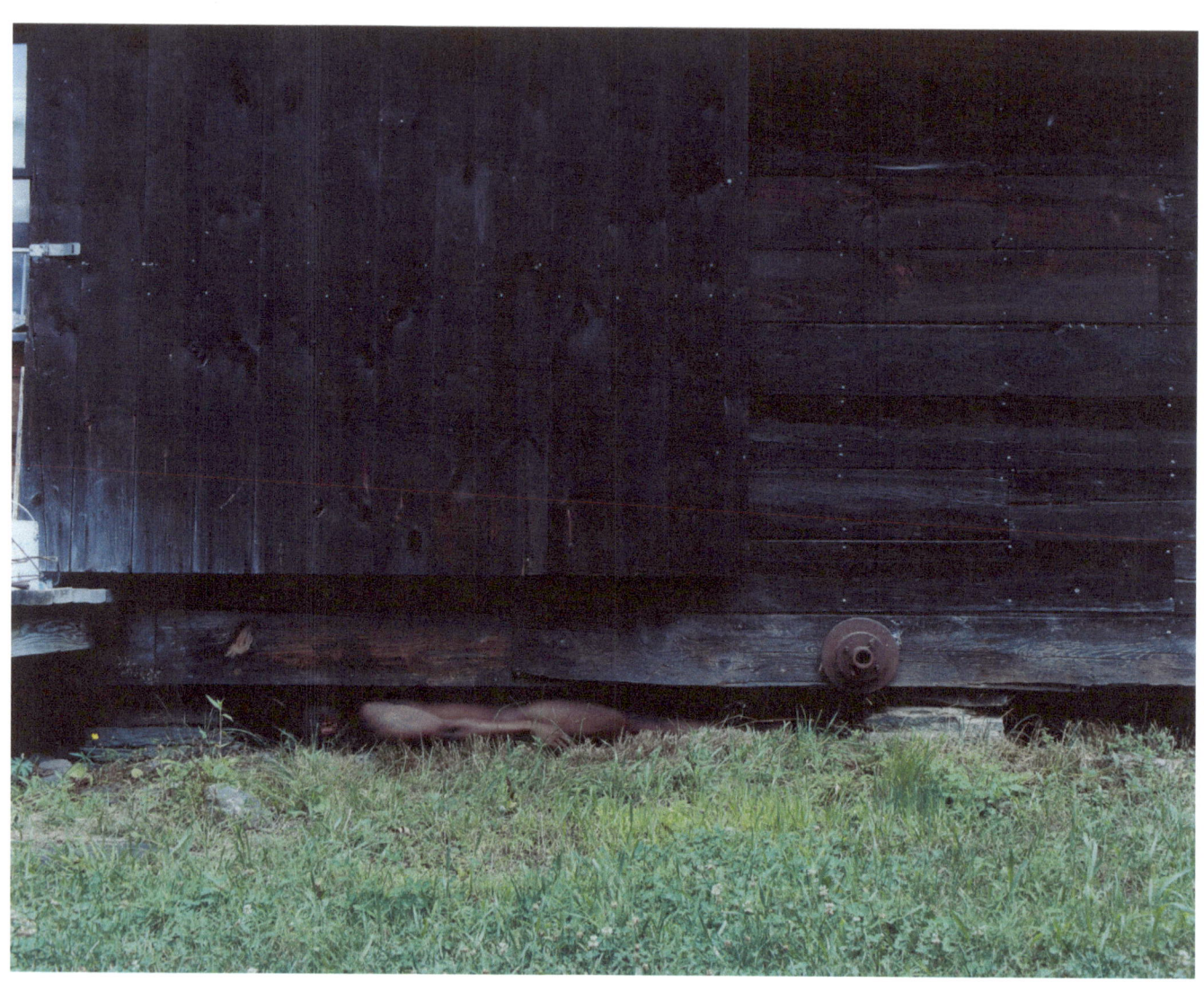

DAWIT L. PETROS
(b. Eritrea, 1972)
Support Structure As Me (from the series "Mimesis"), 2007
Chromogenic color prints
2 parts, 19 ½ x 23 ¾ in. each
The Center for Photography at Woodstock
Permanent Print Collection 2014.009–010

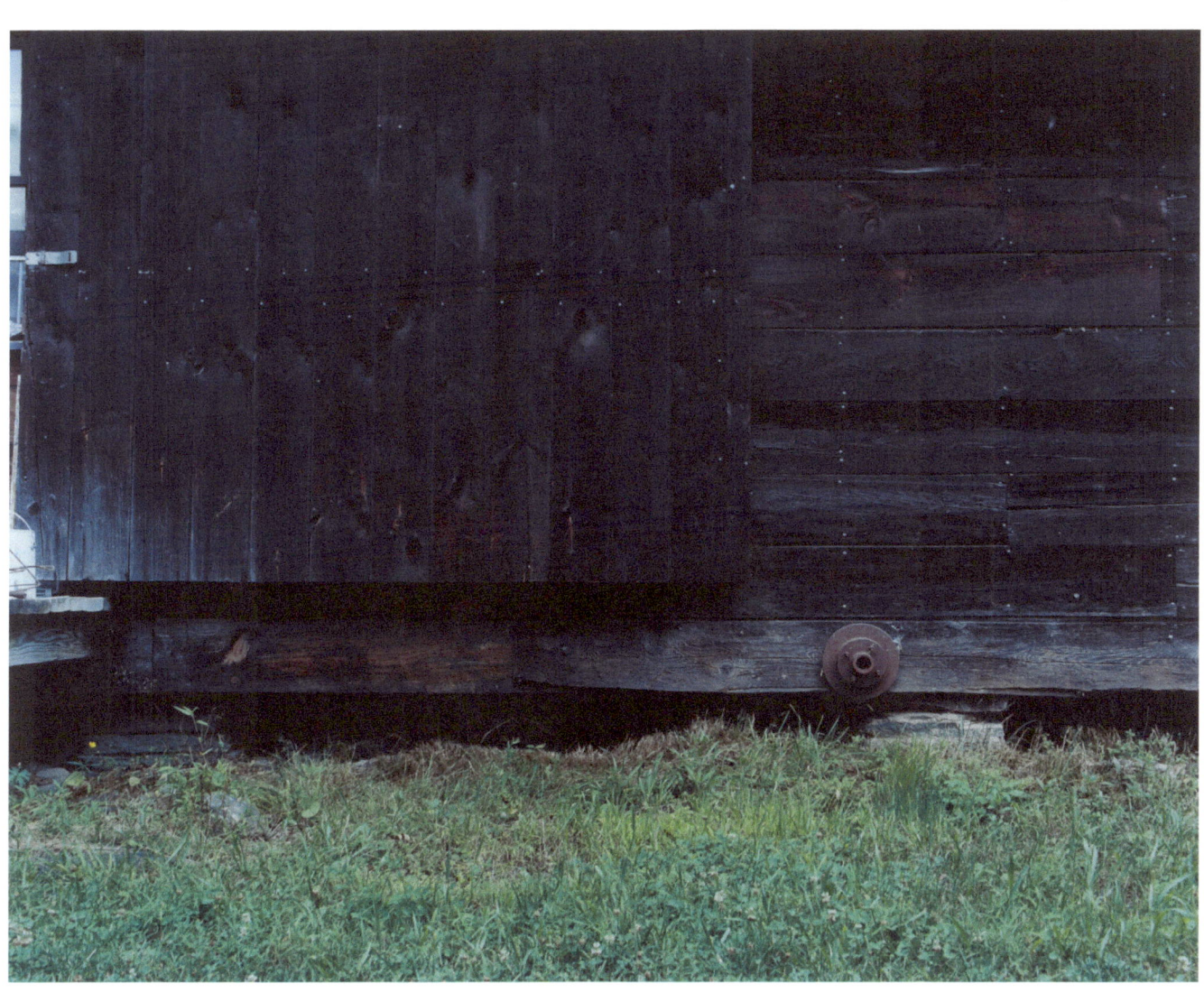

TIM PORTLOCK
(b. United States, 1969)
Garden #16 (from the series "Ghost City"), 2010
Archival pigment print
51 x 68 in.
Courtesy the artist

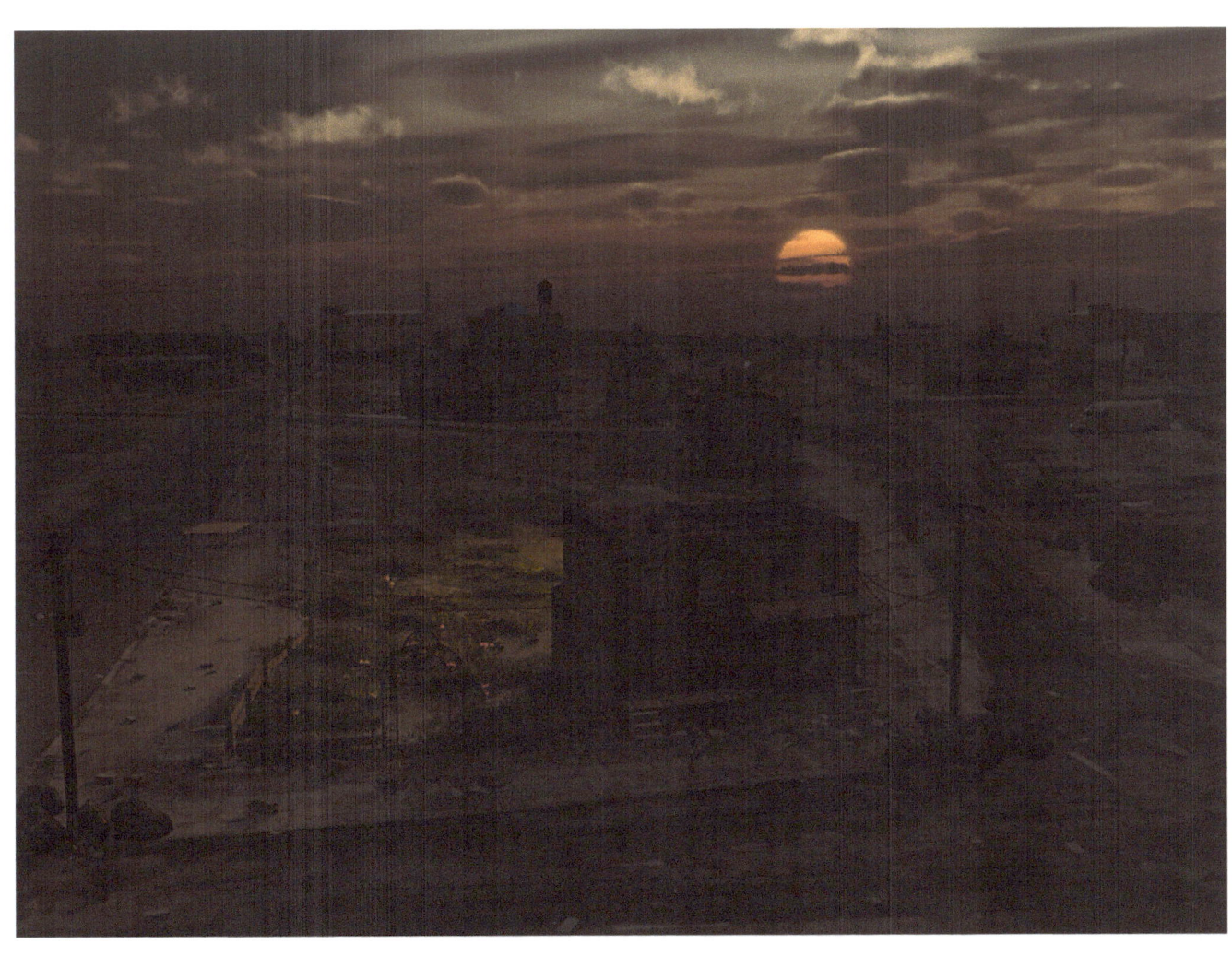

PAUL MPAGI SEPUYA
(b. United States, 1982)
Self-Portrait After
(from the series "Glasco Turnpike"), 2010
Archival pigment print
21 ⅛ x 16 in.
The Center for Photography at Woodstock
Permanent Print Collection 2010.111

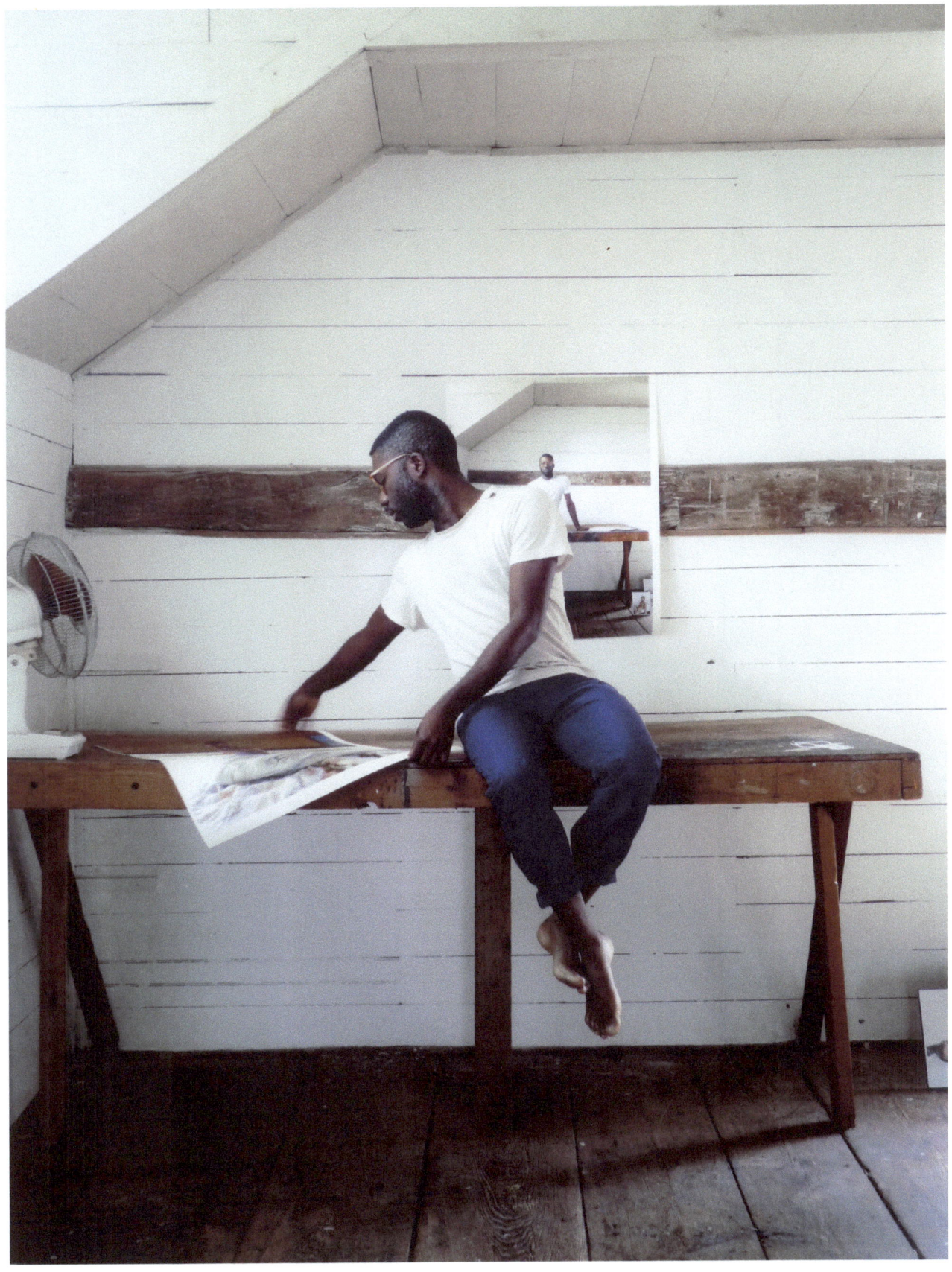

XAVIERA SIMMONS
(b. United States, 1974)
Untitled #6 (from the series "American Book Covers"),
2007
Chromogenic color print
29 ½ x 39 ⅝ in.
The Center for Photography at Woodstock
Permanent Print Collection 2011.003

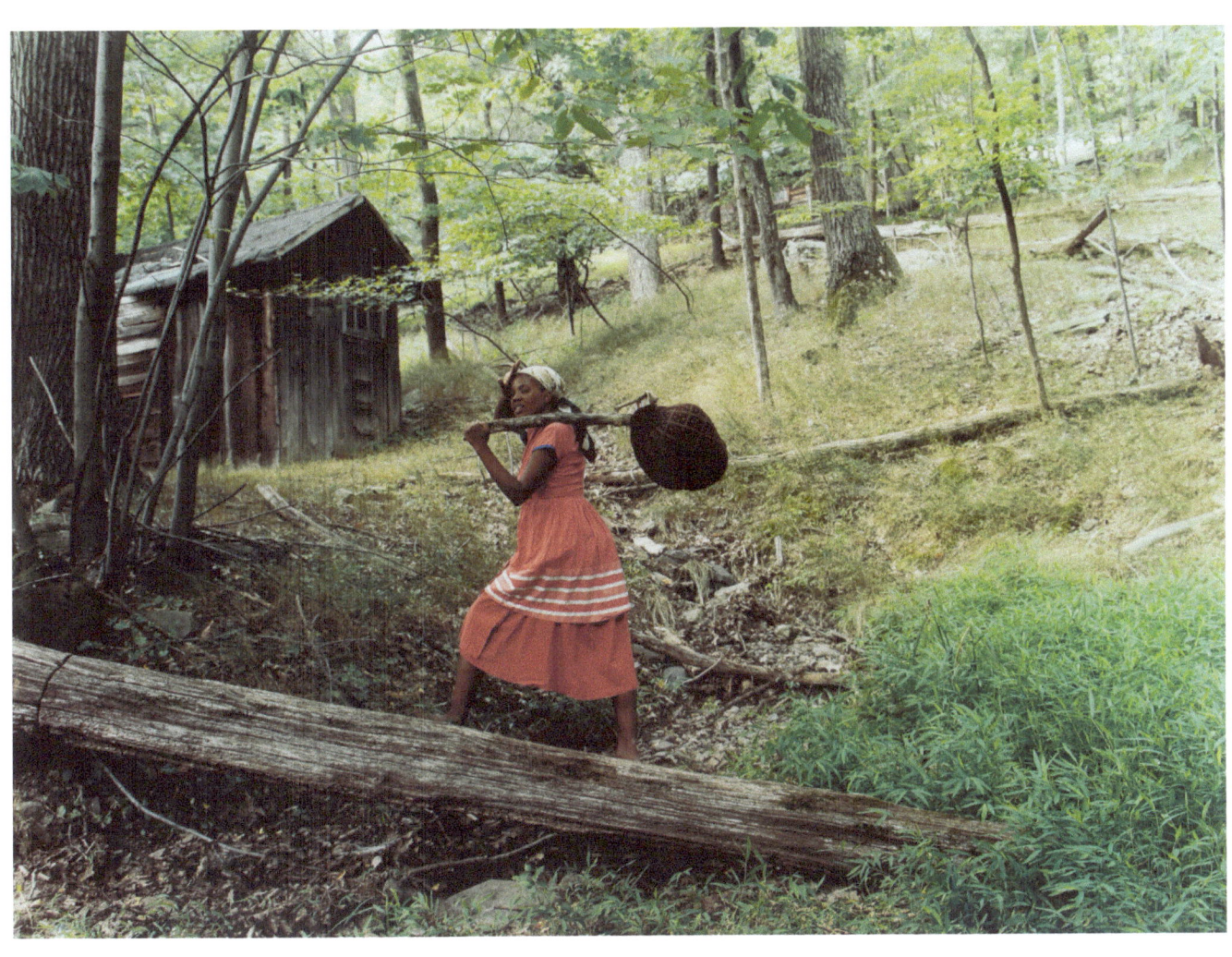

JOANNA TAM
(b. Hong Kong, 1972)
Untitled (from the series "Manner of Delivery"), 2013
Archival pigment print
22 x 32 ⅞ in.
The Center for Photography at Woodstock
Permanent Print Collection 2013.010

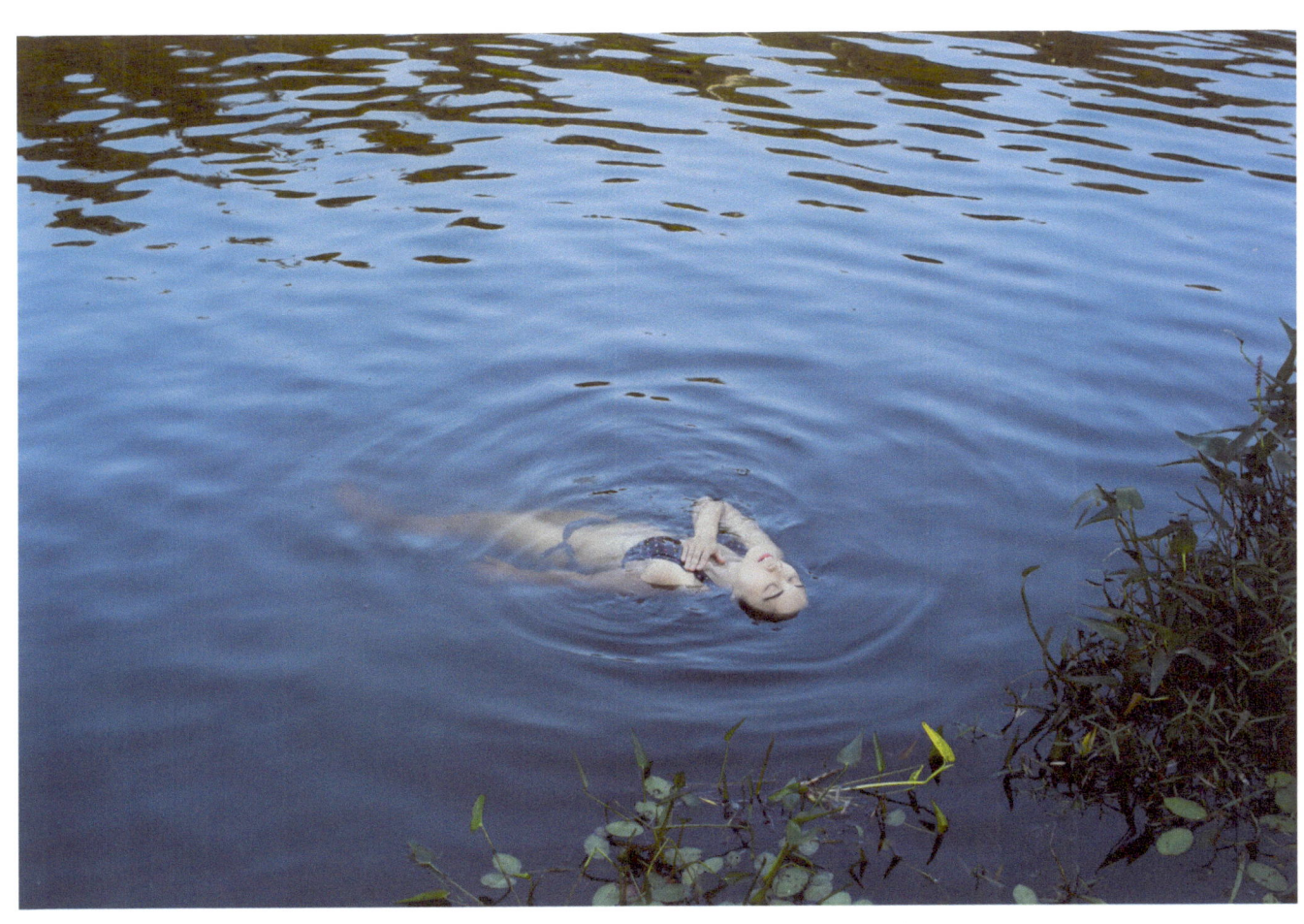

JOANNA TAM
(b. Hong Kong, 1972)
Untitled (from the series "Manner of Delivery"), 2013
Archival pigment print
22 x 32⅞ in.
The Center for Photography at Woodstock
Permanent Print Collection 2013.011

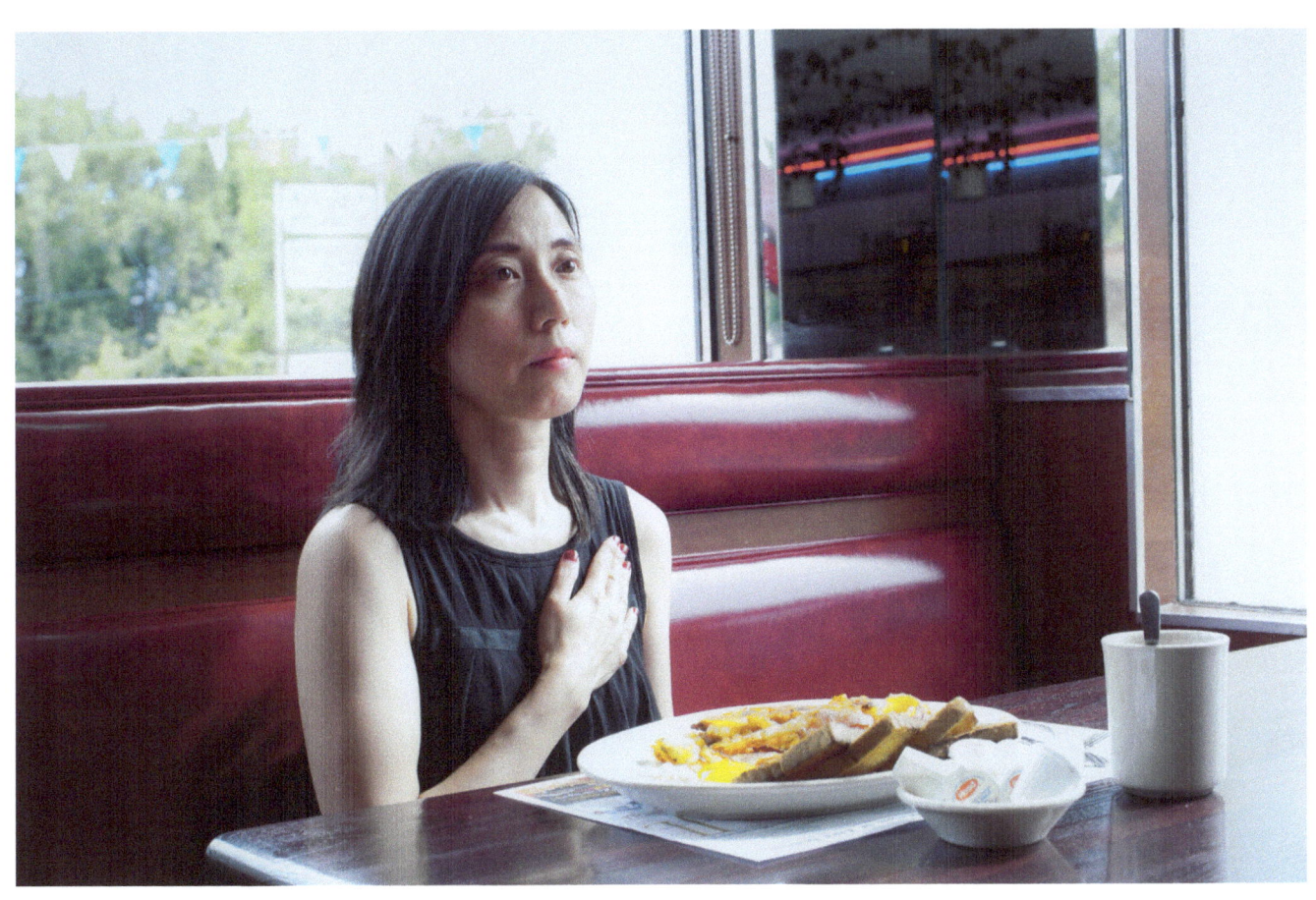

PRESTON WADLEY
(b. United States, 1952)
Letters from Home (from the series "Pentimento"), 2005
Hardcover book, model paint, inkjet print,
plastic molded letters, glue
9 ½ x 13 ¼ x 1 ⅛ in. (open)
The Center for Photography at Woodstock
Permanent Print Collection 2009.035

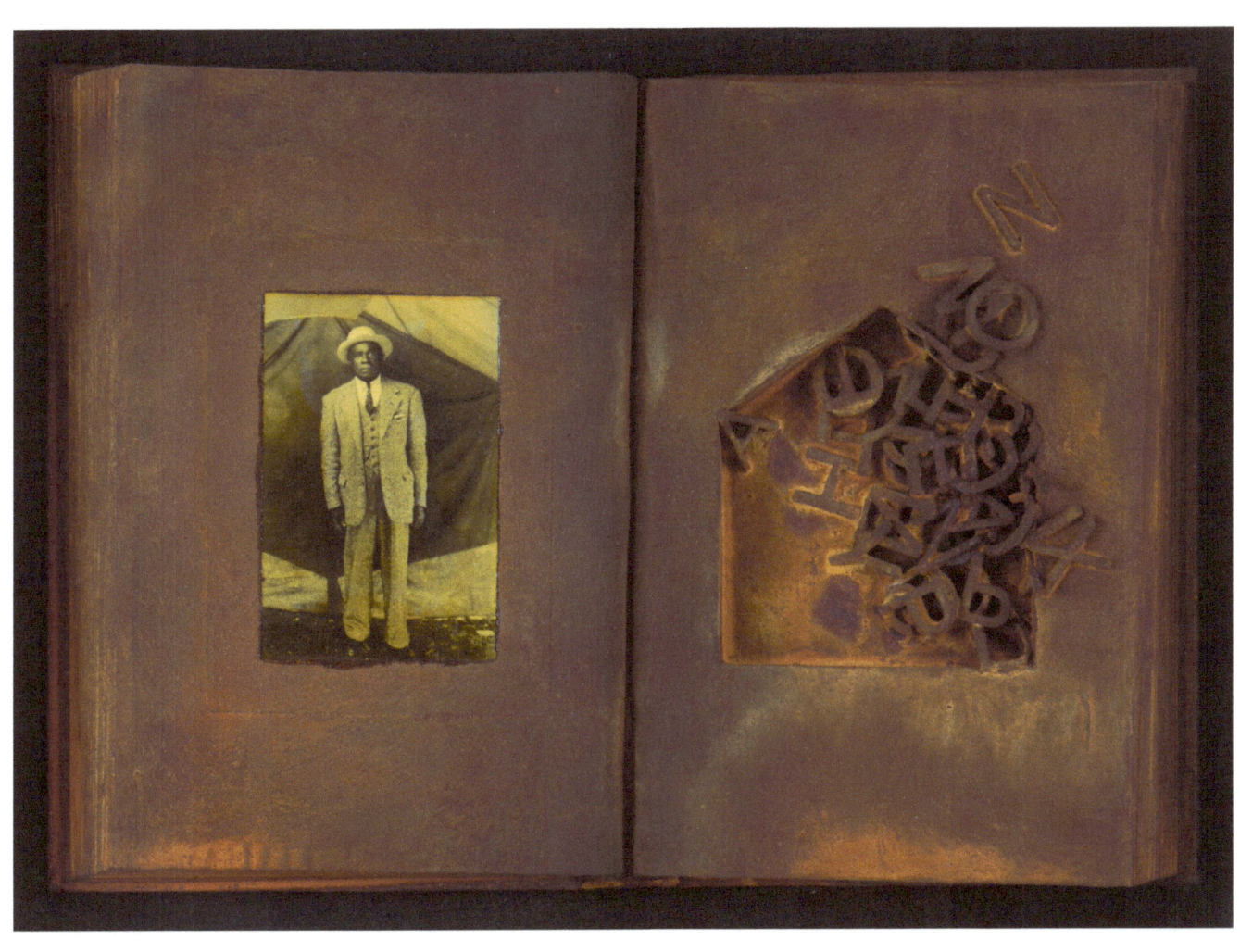

EXHIBITION CHECKLIST

Note: all dimensions are image size unless otherwise noted

ENDIA BEAL
(b. United States, 1985)
9 to 5, 2014
HD video, sound
3 min.
The Center for Photography at Woodstock
Permanent Print Collection 2014.013

WILLIAM CORDOVA
(b. Peru, 1971)
Albany/Peekskill (from the series "chapters: making the invisible visible"), 2007
Archival pigment prints
14 parts, 14 ¼ in. x 13 ft. 5 in. overall
The Center for Photography at Woodstock
Permanent Print Collection 2014.012

ISAAC DIGGS
(b. United States, 1972)
Untitled (Couple at Table), 2011
Archival pigment print
13 x 19 ¼ in.
The Center for Photography at Woodstock
Permanent Print Collection 2011.004

CALEB FERGUSON
(b. United States, 1986)
Untitled, 2012
Archival pigment print
8 x 12 in.
The Center for Photography at Woodstock
Permanent Print Collection 2014.006

CALEB FERGUSON
(b. United States, 1986)
Untitled, 2012
Archival pigment print
8 x 12 in.
The Center for Photography at Woodstock
Permanent Print Collection 2014.003

LATOYA RUBY FRAZIER
(b. United States, 1982)
Momme (from the series "The Notion of Family: Family Work 2002–2008"), 2008
Gelatin silver print
14 ⅝ x 18 ¼ in.
The Center for Photography at Woodstock
Permanent Print Collection 2010.096

LATOYA RUBY FRAZIER
(b. United States, 1982)
Untitled (from the series "The Notion of Family: Family Work 2002–2008"), 2008
Gelatin silver print
14 ⅜ x 19 in.
The Center for Photography at Woodstock
Permanent Print Collection 2010.097

NIKITA GALE
(b. United States, 1983)
1961, 2012
Artist book
9 x 6 ½ x 1 ⅜ in. (closed)
The Center for Photography at Woodstock
Permanent Print Collection 2012.016

GERARD H. GASKIN
(b. Trinidad and Tobago, 1969)
Latex Ball, Manhattan, NY, 2007
(from the series "Legendary"), 2011
Archival pigment print
14 x 21 in.
The Center for Photography at Woodstock
Permanent Print Collection 2011.009

EYAKEM GULILAT
(b. Ethiopia, 1976)
Memories of My Father
(from the series "Memories"), 2010
Archival pigment print
16 x 20 in.
The Center for Photography at Woodstock
Permanent Print Collection 2011.011

TOMMY KHA
(b. United States, 1988)
Little Polite (A Role Study), 2011
Chromogenic color print
21 ⅛ x 28 ¾ in.
The Center for Photography at Woodstock
Permanent Print Collection 2012.007

KATHYA MARIA LANDEROS
(b. United States, 1977)
Verdant Land, 2013
Artist book
13 ⅜ x 16 x ⅝ in. (closed)
The Center for Photography at Woodstock
Permanent Print Collection 2013.007

DEANA LAWSON
(b. United States, 1979)
Daonne, 2012
Archival pigment print
31 x 40 in.
The Center for Photography at Woodstock
Permanent Print Collection 2012.017

ALMA LEIVA
(b. Honduras, 1975)
Celdas #12 (from the series "Celdas (Prison
Cells)"), 2012
Chromogenic color print
23 ¼ x 23 ¼ in.
The Center for Photography at Woodstock
Permanent Print Collection 2014.011

YIJUN PIXY LIAO
(b. China, 1979)
Pimo Dictionary, 2010
Artist book
6 ⅜ x 4 ¾ x ⅞ in. (closed)
The Center for Photography at Woodstock
Permanent Print Collection 2010.113

GINA OSTERLOH
(b. United States, 1973)
Untitled, 2011
Archival pigment prints
3 parts, 19 ¼ x 23 ¾ in. each
The Center for Photography at Woodstock
Permanent Print Collection 2012.010–012

DAWIT L. PETROS
(b. Eritrea, 1972)
Support Structure As Me (from the series
"Mimesis"), 2007
Chromogenic color prints
2 parts, 19 ½ x 23 ¾ in. each
The Center for Photography at Woodstock
Permanent Print Collection 2014.009–010

TIM PORTLOCK
(b. United States, 1969)
Garden #16 (from the series "Ghost City"), 2010
Archival pigment print
51 x 68 in.
Courtesy the artist

PAUL MPAGI SEPUYA
(b. United States, 1982)
Self-Portrait After
(from the series "Glasco Turnpike"), 2010
Archival pigment print
21 ⅛ x 16 in.
The Center for Photography at Woodstock
Permanent Print Collection 2010.111

XAVIERA SIMMONS
(b. United States, 1974)
Untitled #6 (from the series "American Book
Covers"), 2007
Chromogenic color print
29 ½ x 39 ⅝ in.
The Center for Photography at Woodstock
Permanent Print Collection 2011.003

JOANNA TAM
(b. Hong Kong, 1972)
Untitled (from the series "Manner of Delivery"),
2013
Archival pigment print
22 x 32 ⅞ in.
The Center for Photography at Woodstock
Permanent Print Collection 2013.010

JOANNA TAM
(b. Hong Kong, 1972)
Untitled (from the series "Manner of Delivery"),
2013
Archival pigment print
22 x 32 ⅞ in.
The Center for Photography at Woodstock
Permanent Print Collection 2013.011

PRESTON WADLEY
(b. United States, 1952)
Letters from Home (from the series "Pentimento"),
2005
Hardcover book, model paint, inkjet print,
plastic molded letters, glue
9 ½ x 13 ¼ x 1 ⅛ in. (open)
The Center for Photography at Woodstock
Permanent Print Collection 2009.035

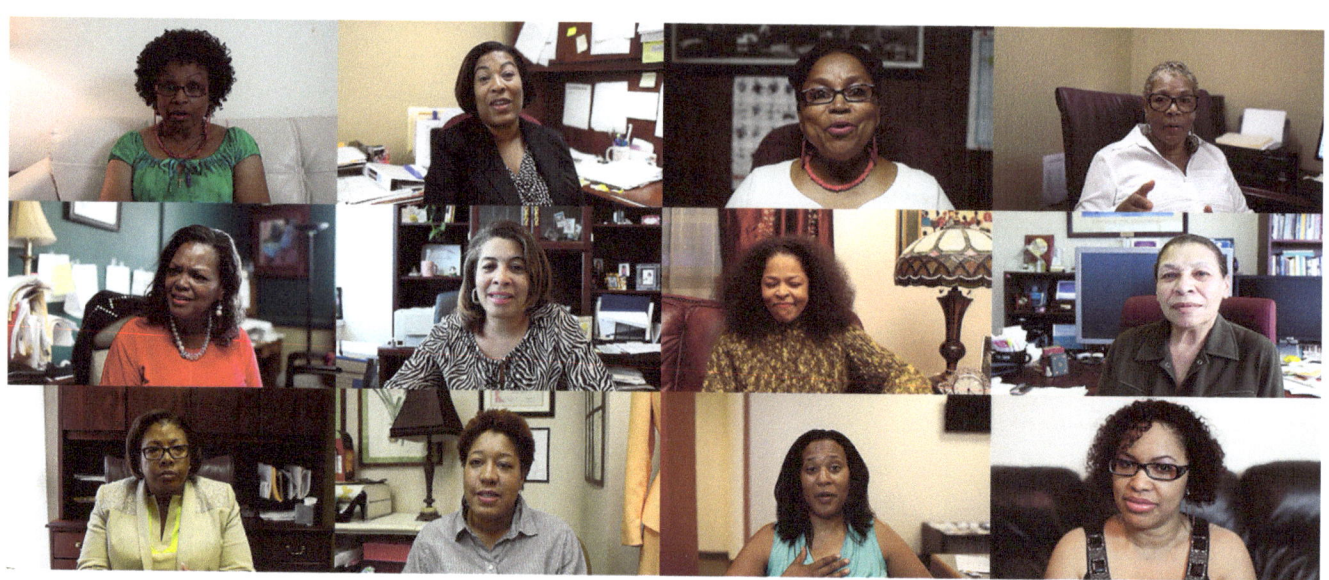

ENDIA BEAL
9 to 5 (stills), 2014

BACK COVER:
JOANNA TAM
Untitled (from the series "Manner of Delivery"), 2013